my **revision** notes

EDEXCEL GCSE

RELIGIOUS STUDIES: CATHOLIC CHRISTIANITY
SPECIFICATION A

Victor W Watton

HODDER
EDUCATION
AN HACHETTE UK COMPANY

The Publishers would like to thank the following for permission to reproduce copyright material.

Acknowledgements

The Holy Bible, New International Version ®, NIV ®. Copyright © 1973, 1978, 1984, 2011 by Biblica, Inc. ® Used by permission. All rights reserved worldwide; *The Catechism of the Catholic Church* by Geoffrey Chapman, (Continuum, 2002).

Every effort has been made to trace all copyright holders, but if any have been inadvertently overlooked, the Publishers will be pleased to make the necessary arrangements at the first opportunity.

Although every effort has been made to ensure that website addresses are correct at time of going to press, Hodder Education cannot be held responsible for the content of any website mentioned in this book. It is sometimes possible to find a relocated web page by typing in the address of the home page for a website in the URL window of your browser.

Hachette UK's policy is to use papers that are natural, renewable and recyclable products and made from wood grown in sustainable forests. The logging and manufacturing processes are expected to conform to the environmental regulations of the country of origin.

Orders: please contact Bookpoint Ltd, 130 Park Drive, Milton Park, Abingdon, Oxon OX14 4SE. Telephone: (44) 01235 827720. Fax: (44) 01235 400454. Email education@bookpoint.co.uk Lines are open from 9 a.m. to 5 p.m., Monday to Saturday, with a 24-hour message answering service. You can also order through our website: www.hoddereducation.co.uk

ISBN: 9781510404809

© Victor W Watton 2017

First published in 2017 by

Hodder Education,

An Hachette UK Company

Carmelite House

50 Victoria Embankment

London EC4Y 0DZ

www.hoddereducation.co.uk

Impression number   10 9 8 7 6

Year   2021 2020 2019

Cover photo © Shaunl/istockphoto.com; © Getty Images/iStockphoto/Thinkstock

Typeset in India by Integra Software Services

Printed in India

A catalogue record for this title is available from the British Library.

Get the most from this book

Everyone has to decide his or her own revision strategy, but it is essential to review your work, learn it and test your understanding. These Revision Notes will help you to do that in a planned way, topic by topic. Use this book as the cornerstone of your revision and don't hesitate to write in it – personalise your notes and check your progress by ticking off each section as you revise.

Tick to track your progress

Use the revision planner on pages 4–6 to plan your revision, topic by topic. Tick each box when you have:

● revised and understood a topic
● tested yourself
● practised the exam questions and checked your answers online.

You can also keep track of your revision by ticking off each topic heading in the book. You may find it helpful to add your own notes as you work through each topic.

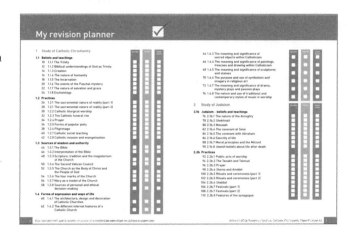

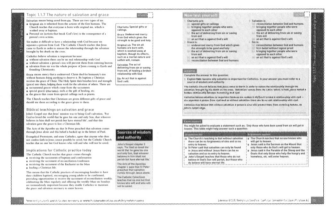

Features to help you succeed

Now test yourself

These short, knowledge-based questions provide the first steps in testing your learning. Answers are provided online.

Definitions and key words

Clear, concise definitions of essential key terms are provided where they first appear.

Sources of wisdom and authority

Knowledge from key religious sources that you can use in the exam.

Activities

These activities will help you to understand each topic in an interactive way. Answers are provided online.

Exam support

Exam support boxes are provided for each topic. Read them to help breakdown exam questions and form useful planning tools for the exam.

Online

Go online to check your answers to the Now test yourself and Activity questions.

My revision planner

	REVISED	TESTED	EXAM READY
	☐	☐	☐
	☐	☐	☐
	☐	☐	☐
	☐	☐	☐
	☐	☐	☐
	☐	☐	☐

2   Study of Judaism

2.1b   Judaism – beliefs and teachings

2.2b   Practices

	REVISED	TESTED	EXAM READY
	☐	☐	☐
	☐	☐	☐
	☐	☐	☐
	☐	☐	☐
	☐	☐	☐
	☐	☐	☐
	☐	☐	☐
	☐	☐	☐
	☐	☐	☐
	☐	☐	☐
	☐	☐	☐
	☐	☐	☐
	☐	☐	☐
	☐	☐	☐
	☐	☐	☐
	☐	☐	☐
	☐	☐	☐

3 Philosophy and ethics based on Catholic Christianity

REVISED | TESTED | EXAM READY

Now test yourself and Activities answers at
www.hoddereducation.co.uk/myrevisionnotes

How to use this book

This book is a revision guide for the Edexcel GCSE Religious Studies Specification A: Area of Study 1 Study of Catholic Christianity, Area of Study 2 Study of second religion Judaism, Area of Study 3 Philosophy and ethics based on Catholic Christianity.

Each chapter is one of the eight sections of the GCSE specification and is divided into the eight topics of the specification. Each topic has the main points you need to know. In the margin is a box with the specialist terms that you may find useful. Under this is another box with some sources of authority which you will need to learn for the c) questions.

On the opposite page are three sections aimed at improving your exam performance (answers are found online):

- Now test yourself is a set of multiple choice questions. You won't have multiple choice questions in the exam but these will help you check your knowledge.
- Each activity is in two parts. Part 1 is a typical a) question which has been started and you need to complete. Part 2 is a typical c) question which you need to complete. These activities provide you with guidance to give you an idea of what is expected in the exam.
- Exam support sets out arguments for and against the issues raised by the topic to make it easier for you to answer the evaluation questions. But remember that in the exam, you will need to evaluate the arguments and write a conclusion about the issue to get more than half of the marks available.

How the assessment works

Area of Study 1 is assessed by an examination lasting 1 hour 45 minutes, which has four questions, one on each section of the specification.

Area of Study 2 is assessed by a 50-minute examination, which has two questions, one on each section of the specification.

Area of Study 3 is assessed by a 50-minute examination, which has two questions, one on each section of the specification.

All the questions follow the same format, that is they are divided into four sub-questions.

Part a) questions

These assess knowledge and might ask you to outline facts, for example 'Outline three Catholic Christian beliefs about marriage.' Each outline will gain you a mark. You should spend no more than 4 minutes answering these questions.

Example:

'Catholic Christians believe that marriage is a sacrament (*one correct belief = 1 mark*).

They believe that marriage is for life (*two correct beliefs = 2 marks*) and that marriage should be between one man and one woman (*three correct beliefs = 3 marks*).'

Part b) questions

These assess understanding and will usually ask you to explain, for example 'Explain two reasons why the Trinity is important to Christians.' There will be 1 mark for each reason and a second mark for developing it. You should spend no more than 5 minutes answering these questions.

Example:

'Catholic Christians feel that the Trinity helps them understand how God works in the world (*1 mark*) through the three persons of the Father who creates, the Son who saves from sin, the Spirit who empowers (*development: 2 marks*). They also believe it helps them understand God's unity (*3 marks*). There are three persons but there is only one substance – God, the three in one (*development: 4 marks*).'

Part c) questions

These also ask you to explain two reasons, but they require you to refer to a source of wisdom and authority, for example 'Explain two reasons why Catholic teachings about sexual relationships are important today. In your answer you must refer to a source of wisdom and authority.' There will be 1 mark for each reason and a second mark for developing it, plus an extra mark for referring to a source of wisdom and authority. You should spend no more than 6 minutes answering these questions.

Example:

Catholic teachings are important because many people today think sex before marriage and cohabitation are alright, but the Catholic Church says they are wrong (1 mark for a reason) *because of the teachings on sexual ethics in the Bible such as Saint Paul condemning sexual immorality in 1 Corinthians* (2 marks for development). *Also the Catechism of the Catholic Church says that `the sexual act must take place exclusively within marriage' and that cohabitation is wrong* (+1 mark for reference to a source of wisdom and authority). *The teachings are also important because many people nowadays think homosexuality is acceptable, but Catholics believe homosexual feelings are acceptable, but homosexual acts are wrong because they are condemned in the Bible* (4 marks), *Saint Paul says in his letter to the Romans that homosexual acts are `shameful lusts'* (5 marks).

Part d) questions

These questions require you to make a reasoned evaluation of a controversial statement by looking at arguments for and against to decide whether the statement is true. To answer these questions, you should:
- Read the bullet points under the statement carefully to see whether you need to refer to two different points of view among Christians (you could refer to Protestants and Catholics), or two different points of view among Catholics, or two different points of view among Jews (you could refer to Reform and Orthodox). If the question asks you to refer to non-religious points of view, you should use a Catholic point of view and non-religious points of view
- When you have decided how the question wants you to evaluate the statement, you need to analyse the validity of the arguments used by those who would agree with the statement (i.e. explain whether and why each reason is convincing)

- Next analyse the validity of the arguments used by people who disagree (i.e. explaining whether and why each reason is convincing)
- **Most importantly you must then come to a conclusion that your analysis has led you to** by making a reasoned judgement about the statement on the basis of what you consider to be the most convincing set of arguments
- It is possible that the arguments are evenly balanced because there are good points on each side, in which case you should conclude with something like the following example. 'The arguments are evenly balanced and the truth of the statement will depend on the beliefs of the person looking at it. Most Catholic Christians would think the statement is correct because they believe in the Magisterium of the Church and so they think that … However, many Protestant Christians would think the statement is incorrect because they believe in the primacy of the Bible and so they think that … '
- **Never use bullet points in d) question answers.**

Strong arguments are likely to use sources of authority:
- Based on what a holy book (Bible, Torah, Tenakh) says
- Based on what the official teachings say (Creeds, Catechism, Mishneh, Talmud, Halakhah, Thirteen Principles)
- Based on what religious leaders say (Papal Encyclicals, decisions of Church Synods, conferences of bishops etc, advice of rabbis)
- Based on scientific evidence
- Based on the laws of a country
- Based on UN Declaration of Human Rights.

Weak arguments are likely to be:
- Based on personal opinion
- Based on someone's interpretation of a religious text
- Based on what everybody thinks/popular ideas
- Based on a minority view in a religion
- Ignorant of religious teachings.

You should spend no more than 12 minutes answering these questions.

Example: 'Catholics must care for the world.'

Evaluate this statement considering arguments for and against.

In your response you should:
- refer to Catholic teachings
- reach a justified conclusion.

Most Catholics have strong arguments for thinking this statement is correct because it is what the Magisterium of the Catholic Church teaches, which is the ultimate source of authority for Catholics. The Catechism teaches that Christians should regard the whole of creation as a gift from God to be used by humans in the way in which God intended. God has given humans control of the earth but only as God's stewards who are responsible for completing the work of creation. The Catechism teaches that Christians have a responsibility to look after God's creation and pass it on to future generations in a better state than they received it. This is a very strong argument for Catholics caring for the world because the Catechism is the official teaching of the Church, the Magisterium, which all Catholics should follow.

Another strong reason for Catholics to care for the world is because both Pope Benedict XVI and Pope Francis have said in encyclicals that Catholics have a duty to protect the environment and to reduce the effects of climate change. As Catholics believe that the Pope is the Head of the Church who has been chosen by God to succeed St Peter, their advice should be followed by Catholics. This is clearly a strong argument for Catholics to care for the world because the authority of the Pope is the basis of Catholicism.

Admittedly, there are some Catholics who would argue that it is more important for Catholics to care for God than to care for the world. They would argue that the first of the Ten Commandments is to love God and that a life of contemplation of God, and praying to God, is more important than the material world. The Contemplative Orders of monks and nuns are often enclosed and cut themselves off from the world so as not to be distracted from God. This is a fairly strong argument because Jesus himself said that loving God was the first and greatest commandment.

Jesus also said that the second commandment was to love your neighbour as yourself and so some Catholics might argue that it is more important to care for people than to care for the world as the second command was to love your neighbour. These are strong arguments for Catholics because they were given by Jesus, who Catholics believe was God's Son and the founder of the Church.

However, these arguments seem to be an interpretation. Surely, caring for the world is the best way to love your neighbour because your neighbour depends on the world being in a good state. It is difficult to love God without loving and caring for the world he has made. Also, if we do not care for the world, life will become much more difficult for humans and so we can only love our neighbour if we care for God's world, therefore Catholics must care for the world.

The part d) questions for Sections 1 and 3 also have three marks for spelling, punctuation and grammar:

- 1 mark is awarded for candidates who spell and punctuate with reasonable accuracy, use rules of grammar to control meaning and use a limited range of specialist terms
- 2 marks are awarded for candidates who spell and punctuate with considerable accuracy, use rules of grammar with general control of meaning overall and use a good range of specialist terms
- 3 marks are awarded for candidates who spell and punctuate with consistent accuracy, use rules of grammar with effective control of meaning and use a wide range of specialist terms.

The sample answer above would be awarded 3 marks because spelling, punctuation and grammar are correct, meaning is clear and a wide range of specialist vocabulary (Catechism, stewards, love of neighbour, encyclical, Pope Francis, Pope Benedict, Ten Commandments, contemplation of God, Contemplative Orders) is used appropriately.

Sources of wisdom and authority do not need exact quotes or references to chapter and verse. You can use a wide range of sources, but

- Sources of wisdom and authority for Catholic Christianity might include: the Bible, the Creeds, the Catholic Catechism, Papal Encyclicals, other statements by the Pope, pastoral advice from bishops.
- Sources of wisdom and authority for Judaism might include: Torah, Tenakh, Mishneh, Talmud, Mitzvot, Thirteen Principles of Faith, Pirke Avot, decisions of Bet Din, advice from great rabbis.

See the specification for all sources of wisdom and authority.

The activities after each topic give you a chance to practise the a) and c) questions with some help. The exam support after each topic gives you ideas for arguments for and against in the d) questions, but you must write your own evaluation and conclusion at the end of your answer.

(Pearson Education accepts no responsibility whatsoever for the accuracy or method of working in the answers given above.)

1.1 Beliefs and teachings

Topic 1.1.1 The Trinity

Christians worship only one God because:
- it is the teaching of the Bible
- Jesus taught that there is only one God
- God's Unity is the teaching of the **magisterium**, the **creeds** and the **Catechism**.

The **Nicene Creed** explains that this one God exists as three persons – the Father, Son and Holy Spirit – who are all equal and all eternal.

Believing in God the Father means Catholics believe:
- a Christian's relationship with God should be like a child's relationship with its father
- God has a continuing relationship of love and care with his creation.
- God will provide for and protect his people because he is 'our Father'.

Believing in God the Son shows Catholics believe:
- Jesus is God who has become a human being
- Christians can worship Jesus because he is God
- Jesus was conceived by the action of the Holy Spirit (the virgin birth).

Believing in God the Holy Spirit shows Catholics believe that the Holy Spirit
- is the means by which God communicates with humans
- inspired the Bible
- is the means by which God helps the Church preserve and explain Christ's teachings
- is the means by which all the **sacraments** of the Church put believers into communion with Christ.

How the Trinity is reflected in worship and belief
- Every Mass beginning with a welcome in the name of the Trinity.
- Worshippers stating their belief in the Trinity in the Nicene Creed in the Mass.
- The Trinity is the main belief of the Nicene Creed.
- Belief in God the Holy Spirit helps Christians understand the presence of God in the world.

How belief in the Trinity is reflected in the life of a Catholic today
- Praying to the Father, through the Son, in the power and presence of the Holy Spirit gives Catholics the spiritual sense of God as 'beyond us, with us and in us'.
- The Trinity gives Catholics the sense that God is active and present in the world as Father, Son and Holy Spirit.
- The Trinity teaches Catholics they must work together to bring God's love into the world, just as the persons of the Holy Trinity work together to bring God's love into the world.

Catechism The official teaching of the Catholic Church.

Creed Statement of Christian beliefs.

Magisterium The Pope and bishops interpreting the Bible and tradition for Catholics today.

Nicene Creed Statement of Christian belief accepted by most Christians.

Sacraments Outward signs of an inward blessing through which invisible grace is given to a person.

Sources of wisdom and authority

The Catechism says that the Trinity is a holy mystery central to the Christian faith.

The Nicene Creed states that the Trinity is one God experienced as Father, Son and Holy Spirit.

The Catechism says that belief in only one God is the basis of Christianity.

Now test yourself

1 The Nicene Creed is:
  (a) The agreed statement of Christian belief
  (b) A statement about Christian beliefs
  (c) A statement of Christian belief agreed by Catholic and Orthodox
  (d) A statement about the Trinity
2 Monotheism is:
  (a) Belief in God
  (b) Belief in the Christian God
  (c) Belief in one God
  (d) Belief in many gods
3 The official teaching of the Catholic Church is known as:
  (a) Salvation
  (b) Sin
  (c) Catechism
  (d) Eucharist
4 The Pope and bishops interpreting the Bible and Tradition for Catholics today is called:
  (a) Catechism
  (b) Apostolic Tradition
  (c) Magisterium
  (d) Encyclicals

Activities

Complete the answers to these questions:
1 Outline **three** ways belief in the Trinity is shown in Catholic worship.

Catholics show their belief in the Trinity when they repeat the Nicene Creed at the Mass. Another way is in every mass beginning (starts) with a welcome in the name of the Trinity.

Another way is
belief in God the Holy Spirit helps Christians understand the presence of God in the world

2 Explain **two** things Catholic Christians believe about the Trinity. In your answer you must refer to a source of wisdom and authority.

Catholic Christians believe that although God is one, God is experienced as a Trinity: God the Father, God the Son and God the Holy Spirit. The Nicene Creed explains that this one God exists as three persons - the Father, Son and Holy Spirit - who are all equal and all eternal.

Exam support

You might be asked to evaluate a statement such as: *'You can't be a Christian if you don't believe in the Trinity.'* This table might help answer such a question:

Arguments for	Arguments against
● The Nicene Creed contains a statement of belief in the Trinity. ● The Catechism of the Catholic Church says the Trinity is central to Christian belief and life. ● Churches can be members of the World Council of Churches only if they believe in the Trinity.	● Jesus said the most important things were to love God and love your neighbour. ● Christians such as Mormons and Unitarians do not believe in the Trinity. ● Jesus said, 'by their fruits shall you know them', that is, what you do is more important than what you believe.

Topic 1.1.2 Biblical understandings of God as Trinity — links.

The threefold nature of God is hinted at in the Old Testament:

- In Genesis, God speaks the Word to create and the Spirit hovers over creation.
- The prophet Isaiah claims that God sends his Word and Spirit to create and guide.

God as the Trinity is clearly referred to in the New Testament:

- Jesus' final words in Matthew are to make disciples, baptising them in the name of the Father and of the Son and of the Holy Spirit.
- St Paul makes several references to the Trinity in his letters.
- St Peter begins his first letter with a reference to the Trinity.

The Gospel accounts of the baptism of Jesus clearly show that God is the Trinity:

- God the Son goes into the Jordan to be baptised.
- As he is being baptised, God the Holy Spirit descends like a dove and rests on him.
- God the Father speaks from heaven, announcing that this is his beloved Son.

So at the very beginning of Jesus' ministry – his teaching and his miracles – there is a statement that the Father, the Son and the Holy Spirit are at work as the one God in his ministry.

Belief in God as a Trinity of persons is important for Catholics because the Trinity helps Catholics understand the different ways that God has shown his presence in the world:

- God the Father helps Catholics understand God's power and creativity and his care for the world and its peoples.
- God the Son helps Catholics understand the love of God, the sacrifice of God leading to salvation from sin and the promise of eternal life.
- God the Holy Spirit helps Catholics understand the presence of God in the world and the strength that it brings to Catholics.

Historical development of the doctrine of the Trinity

Several **heresies** arose from debates about the nature of Jesus and the Trinity. The main ones were:

- **Adoptionism**: the belief that Jesus was an ordinary man, born of Joseph and Mary, who became the Christ and Son of God at his baptism when he was 'adopted' by God.
- **Arianism**: the belief that the Son was created by the Father at the beginning of the universe. The Son is therefore a god, but not God.

Church Councils (meetings of bishops representing all areas of the Church) were called to make a final declaration of Christian beliefs on these matters. The Councils of Nicaea (325CE) and Constantinople (381CE) explained the doctrine of the Trinity and formulated the Nicene Creed as a statement of Christian belief about the nature of Jesus and the Trinity.

The Councils of Nicaea and Constantinople are the only ones accepted by all Christians.

Adoptionism The heresy that the Son of God was adopted by God and not begotten of God.

Arianism The heresy that the Son of God was created by God after the creation.

Church Council Assembly of bishops authorised to make decisions on theological issues.

Heresy A religious opinion which contradicts official Church teaching.

Sources of wisdom and authority

In Genesis chapter 1, God speaks the Word to create and the Spirit hovers over creation.

Isaiah chapter 59 says that God sends his Word and Spirit to create and guide.

Jesus' final words in Matthew tell the disciples to baptise converts in the name of the Father and of the Son and of the Holy Spirit.

St Paul says in 2 Corinthians 'May the grace of our Lord Jesus Christ, and the love of God, and the fellowship of the Holy Spirit be with you all'.

Now test yourself

1 The idea that the Son of God was adopted by God and not begotten of God is:
   (a) Heresy
   (b) Arianism
   (c) Adoptionism ✓
   (d) Nicene

2 The idea that the Son of God was created by God after the creation is:
   (a) Heresy
   (b) Arianism ✓
   (c) Adoptionism
   (d) Nicene

3 An assembly of bishops authorised to make decisions on theological issues is a:
   (a) Church Assembly
   (b) Church Convocation
   (c) Church Council ✓
   (d) Church Synod

4 A religious opinion which contradicts official Church teaching is a:
   (a) Doctrine
   (b) Heresy ✓
   (c) Creed
   (d) Catechism

Activities

Complete the answers to these questions:

1 Outline **three** features of the development of the doctrine of the Trinity.

One feature is that there were debates in the Church about the nature of the Trinity. Another feature is that these debates led to Trinitarian heresies like Arianism. A third feature is that the Councils of Nicaea and Constantinople settled the problem with the

Church councils by a final declaration of christian beliefs on these matters. They both explained the doctrine of the Trinity and formulated the Nicene Creed as a statement of christian belief of the nature of Jesus and Trinity

2 Explain **two** reasons why belief in the Trinity is important for Catholics. In your answer you must refer to a source of wisdom and authority.

Belief in the Trinity is important for Catholics because Jesus' last words in Matthew's Gospel told Christians to baptise in the name of the Father, and of the Son and of the Holy Spirit.

Another reason is that the Trinity helps Catholics understand the different ways that God has shown his presence in the world:

God the Father helps catholics understand God's power and creativity and his care for the world and its peoples.

Exam support

You might be asked to evaluate a statement such as: 'The decisions of Church Councils 1500 years ago have nothing to do with life in the twenty-first century.' This table might help answer such a question:

Arguments for	Arguments against
• Church Councils then were living in a different world: no computers, no internet, cars, planes, etc. • Church Councils then would have had a different world view — flat Earth, six-day creation, etc. • Church Councils then would have had no idea of the power of science to change the world. • Church Councils then would have had no concept of human rights, democracy, etc.	• The Church teaches that the Councils were inspired and guided by God who does not change. • The Church Councils made decisions about doctrines which are eternally true. • Church Councils were made up of holy people who have things to teach the twenty-first century because of their understanding of God. • Although many things have changed, the basics of life — love, friendship, joy, sorrow, death — have not changed.

The biblical creation

According to Genesis chapter 1, God created the whole universe in six days, starting with the heavens and the Earth and ending with the creation of humans (male and female together). Each part of the creation came about because of God's words, and God made humans to have authority over the world and its contents.

According to Genesis chapters 2–3, God created the heavens and the Earth, then formed Adam, then vegetation, animals and birds, then created Eve from Adam's rib. Adam and Eve lived in the Garden of Eden until the serpent tempted them to eat forbidden fruit to become like God. Eve ate the fruit and gave some to Adam. As a result of this first sin they were banished from the Garden.

The Catholic understanding of Genesis

The Catholic Church believes the Bible writers were inspired by God but expressed things in their own words. So Genesis has two versions of creation to communicate eternal truths about God's purpose and human sinfulness. Catholics accept the scientific view of creation but believe Genesis reveals the truth that creation came from God.

Different Christian views

- **Fundamentalist Protestants** believe the Bible is the word of God and so is true and so Genesis is factually correct. They believe Genesis 1 gives the overall picture of creation, whereas Genesis 2–3 concentrates on Day 6 and **original sin**, needing the salvation of Jesus. They do not accept the **Big Bang** and **evolution**.
- **Mainstream Protestants** believe that the Bible is the Word of God but not his actual words. They see Genesis 2–3 as a commentary on Genesis 1 rather than a different story. They regard Genesis 1 as fairly factual, with the days as billions of years. They accept the Big Bang and evolution.
- **Liberal Protestants** believe that the Bible is people's words about God rather than the words of God. They regard Genesis 1 as a story about creation where what is important is the truth that the universe was created by God. They see Genesis 2–3 as written by a different person. They accept the Big Bang and evolution.

What creation shows about the nature of God

The biblical story of creation shows that God is:
- the Creator who created the heaven and the Earth
- **omnipotent** because he created the universe out of nothing (**ex nihilo**)
- **benevolent** because he created the world for humans and made it a good place for them to live, with all the sustenance they need
- eternal because he had no beginning (to create he must have existed before the beginning of time).

The biblical story also shows that life is sacred. Those things which God creates must be like him, holy, so humans need to treat the creation carefully and with respect.

Benevolent Good and loving.

Big Bang The idea that the universe began from an explosion of matter.

Evolution The idea that life forms change over time and humans have developed from single-cell organisms.

Ex nihilo From nothing.

Omnipotent All powerful.

Original sin The sin of the first humans (symbolised by Adam and Eve) inherited by humans as mortality and selfishness.

Sources of wisdom and authority

'Let us make man in our image, in our likeness, and let them rule over the fish of the sea and the birds of the air, over the livestock, over all the earth' (Genesis 1:26).

Genesis 1 says, 'God saw all that he had made and it was very good.'

The Catechism says that Genesis 1–3 may have different sources, but they come at the beginning of the Bible to express the truth of creation.

Now test yourself

1 A word meaning all-good, all-loving is:
   (a) Benevolent
   (b) Evolution
   (c) Ex nihilo
   (d) Omnipotent

2 The idea that life forms change over time is:
   (a) Benevolent
   (b) Evolution
   (c) Ex nihilo
   (d) Omnipotent

3 A word meaning from nothing is:
   (a) Benevolent
   (b) Evolution
   (c) Ex nihilo
   (d) Omnipotent

4 A word meaning all powerful is:
   (a) Benevolent
   (b) Evolution
   (c) Ex nihilo
   (d) Omnipotent

Activities

Complete the answers to these questions:

1 Outline **three** features of the creation described in Genesis 1.

One feature is that God created everything in six days. Another feature is that God created male and female together. A third feature is

that God made humans to have authority over the world and its contents

2 Explain **two** different interpretations of the accounts of creation in Genesis. In your answer you must refer to a source of wisdom and authority.

Christians who believe the Bible is the literal word of God (literalists) believe that both Genesis 1 and 2 are scientific truth. Chapter 1 gives the overall picture and chapters 2–3 give details of day six. They believe that the scientific idea of Big Bang and evolution is wrong.

Another interpretation is

that liberal protestants believe in people's words about God rather than the words of God. Genesis 1 is a story universe created by God. Genesis 2-3 written by a different person. They accept the Big Bang and evolution.

Exam support

You might be asked to evaluate a statement such as: *'It's hard to believe the biblical accounts of creation.'*
This table might help answer such a question:

Arguments for	Arguments against
● Science shows that the creation of the universe took billions of years, not six days.	● If the Bible is the word of God, then it must be true and so is easy to believe.
● Science shows that humans evolved from other species of mammals, not that they were suddenly created by God.	● It is easier to believe that God created the universe than that this huge complex system was just an accident.
● Science has evidence, such as the Red Shift Effect and the fossil record.	● It is easy to explain the different accounts in Genesis if chapters 2–3 are poetic explanations of chapter 1.
● There are two Bible accounts which seem to contradict one another.	● Genesis 1 is factual when a day is defined as billions of years rather than 24 hours.

Topic 1.1.4 The nature of humanity

Genesis teaches that God created human beings in his image. This does not mean that they look like God, but that they have **free will**, reason and a conscience. They are capable of **self-knowledge**, and have the freedom to choose between good and evil.

This teaching reminds Catholics that:
- each human being is special, unique and sacred in God's sight
- humans are more than animals and are not to be used as objects
- humans have fundamental human rights such as freedom of conscience and expression, a right to food, shelter and health care.

Humanity's relationship with creation

Being made in the image of God gives humans a huge responsibility to care for the planet God has made rather than spoil it.

The Catholic Church teaches that Christians should regard the whole of creation as a gift from God to be used by humans in the way in which God intended. God has given humans control of the Earth and its resources (**dominion**), but only as God's stewards responsible for completing the work of creation.

Stewardship means that Christians have a responsibility to:
- look after God's creation and pass it on to future generations in a better state than they received it
- make sure creation is not exploited by humans, resulting in such things as pollution
- make sure that the earth's resources are shared out fairly
- make sure that humans treat God's creation fairly and harmoniously.

Non-Catholic Christians have the same beliefs about the nature of humanity, and humanity's relationship with creation, as Catholics.

Different understandings of humanity's relationship with creation

- Humanists do not believe in God and are non-religious. They believe in reason and science and that moral principles can be worked out in terms of what will make life better for everyone. Reason and science teach them that people need to care for and look after the planet so that it can provide for future generations.
- Other non-religious people (**atheists** and those who are uninterested in religion) have two views: some think people should work to preserve the environment for the future; others think the world is to be enjoyed by people however they like.

Atheist Someone who believes that God does not exist.

Dominion Having power and authority.

Encyclical A letter addressed by the Pope to all the bishops of the Church.

Free will The idea that human beings are free to make their own choices.

Humanism Belief in reason and human values but no belief in God.

Self-knowledge Knowing who you are and why you are here.

Stewardship Looking after something so it can be passed on to the next generation.

Sources of wisdom and authority

The Catechism of the Catholic Church states that being in the image of God means that humans have dignity because they are not a thing, they are a person.

Genesis 1 says that God gave humans control of the living things on the Earth.

Pope Benedict XVI and Pope Francis have said in **encyclicals** that Catholics have a duty to protect the environment and to reduce the effects of climate change.

The Catechism says that humanity's control of nature is limited by God requiring them to preserve the environment and care for their neighbours.

Now test yourself

1 A letter addressed by the Pope to all the bishops of the Church is:
 (a) Humanism
 (b) Self-knowledge
 (c) Stewardship
 (d) Encyclical

2 Belief in reason and human values but no belief in God is:
 (a) Humanism
 (b) Self-knowledge
 (c) Stewardship
 (d) Encyclical

3 Knowing who you are and why you are here is:
 (a) Humanism
 (b) Self-knowledge
 (c) Stewardship
 (d) Encyclical

4 Looking after something so it can be passed on to the next generation is:
 (a) Humanism
 (b) Self-knowledge
 (c) Stewardship
 (d) Encyclical

Activities

Complete the answers to these questions:

1 Outline **three** things Christians believe about humans being made in the image of God.

One thing Christians believe this means is that humans have free will — they can choose between good and evil. Another thing is that they have reason and so can work things out. A third thing is that humans are capable of

....

2 Explain **two** meanings of stewardship for Catholics. In your answer you must refer to a source of wisdom and authority.

Catholics believe that stewardship means that they have a duty to look after God's creation and pass it on to future generations in a better state than they have received it.

Another meaning is

....

....

Exam support

You might be asked to evaluate a statement such as: *'Climate change would not be a problem if everyone were a Catholic.'* This table might help answer such a question:

Arguments for	Arguments against
● The Catechism says Catholics should look after God's creation and pass it on to future generations in a better state than they received it. ● The Catechism says Catholics should make sure creation is not exploited by humans, resulting in such things as pollution. ● The Catechism says Catholics should make sure that the earth's resources are shared out fairly. ● Pope Benedict and Pope Francis have issued encyclicals asking Catholics to protect the environment and reduce the effects of climate change.	● Catholics are still driving cars so the teachings have not had much effect. ● Catholics do not seem to be using renewable energy sources more than non-Catholics so the teachings have not had much effect. ● At least 50 per cent of Catholics in the USA are climate change deniers.

The Incarnation is the Christian belief that God became a human being in Jesus (Jesus was God incarnate).

As the only Son of God, Catholics believe that Jesus did not have a normal conception but he did have a normal birth. Catholics believe that Mary was a virgin when Jesus was born and remained a virgin throughout her life. They believe that being born of a virgin was the way God became man.

The **virgin birth** is important to all Christians because it shows that:
● Jesus was the Son of God (not just a human being chosen and sent by God)
● God was in him and he was in God
● Jesus had two natures – in his human nature he was a human being, but in his divine nature he was God (fully human and fully divine).

The biblical basis for the Incarnation

Matthew's Gospel tells how Joseph was told by an angel that Mary was a virgin who had conceived by the Holy Spirit and that the child was to be called Jesus because he would save the people from their sins. Joseph then married Mary, Jesus was born in Bethlehem and they were visited by Wise Men.

Luke's Gospel tells how the Angel Gabriel appeared to Mary and told her about the virgin birth of Jesus, who was born and visited by shepherds who had been visited by angels telling them of Jesus' miraculous birth.

John's Gospel records the Incarnation in a **theological** form, identifying Jesus as the Word of God, the second person of the Trinity. John begins his Gospel at the beginning of the universe when the Word made everything that is. He then describes how the Word became flesh (the Incarnation), that is Jesus was God in human form.

There are references to the Incarnation throughout the rest of the New Testament, especially in the letters of St Paul.

Why the Incarnation is important for Catholics

The Incarnation is important for Catholics because:
● it shows that God cared so much for the world that he came to Earth in Jesus to save people from their sins
● in Jesus, the incarnate Word of God, humans can see what God is like
● through the Incarnation, God began the process of **salvation** from sin.

> **Incarnation** The belief that God became a human being as Jesus.
>
> **Salvation** Deliverance from sin and its consequences.
>
> **Theological** Academic study of God and religious ideas.
>
> **Virgin birth** The belief that Jesus was not conceived through sex.

Sources of wisdom and authority

John's Gospel, chapter 1 says that in Jesus, the Word became flesh and made his dwelling among us, showing us the glory of God.

John's Gospel, chapter 1 says that though no one has seen God, the Incarnation has made God known.

St Paul says in Colossians that 'the Son is the image of the invisible God'.

Now test yourself

1 The Incarnation is:
   (a) the belief that God became a human being as Jesus
   (b) deliverance from sin and its consequences
   (c) academic study of God and religious ideas
   (d) the belief that Jesus was not conceived through sex

2 Salvation is:
   (a) the belief that God became a human being as Jesus
   (b) deliverance from sin and its consequences
   (c) academic study of God and religious ideas
   (d) the belief that Jesus was not conceived through sex

3 Theological means:
   (a) the belief that God became a human being as Jesus
   (b) deliverance from sin and its consequences
   (c) academic study of God and religious ideas
   (d) the belief that Jesus was not conceived through sex

4 Virgin birth is:
   (a) the belief that God became a human being as Jesus
   (b) deliverance from sin and its consequences
   (c) academic study of God and religious ideas
   (d) the belief that Jesus was not conceived through sex

Activities

Complete the answers to these questions:

1 Outline **three** Catholic beliefs about the virgin birth.

One Catholic belief about the virgin birth is that, as the only Son of God, Jesus did not have a normal conception but he did have a normal birth. Another belief is that Mary was a virgin when Jesus was born and remained a virgin throughout her life. A third Catholic belief is that being born of a virgin was __the way God became man.__

2 Explain **two** reasons why the Incarnation is important for Catholics. In your answer you must refer to a source of wisdom and authority.

The Incarnation is important for Catholics because in Jesus, the incarnate Word of God, humans can see what God is like. John's Gospel says that in Jesus, the Word became flesh and made his dwelling among us, showing us the glory of God.

Another reason is that the Incarnation shows that God cared so much for the world that __he came to Earth in Jesus to save people from their sins__

Exam support

You might be asked to evaluate a statement such as: *'Jesus was God incarnate.'* This table might help answer such a question:

Arguments for	Arguments against
● Jesus had a virgin birth and only God could be born of a virgin. ● Jesus performed miracles, such as stilling a storm, that only God could do. ● Jesus rose from the dead, which only God could do. ● It is the teaching of all the Christian Churches and creeds.	● The only evidence for the Incarnation is the Bible and there is no reason for believing the Bible is the truth. ● The accounts in Matthew and Luke contradict each other. ● A human being requires male and female genes, so if Jesus was a human being, where did his male genes come from? ● God is supposed to be an infinite being but Jesus was a finite being, which means Jesus could not have been God.

REVISED

The **Paschal mystery** is the term the Church uses to refer to the death and resurrection of Jesus and their effects on salvation.

The Last Supper

The night before he was crucified, Jesus enjoyed a meal with his disciples in Jerusalem when he shared bread and wine with them, saying the bread was his body and the wine his blood, so establishing the Eucharist.

Garden of Gethsemane

After supper, Jesus left the disciples while he went to pray and asked God, 'take this cup from me, yet not my will but yours be done'. When he went back, the disciples were asleep. As they woke, one of them, Judas Iscariot, arrived with the chief priests to arrest Jesus. The disciples wanted to fight, but Jesus wouldn't let them.

The trials

Peter followed but denied he knew Jesus when he was challenged. The **Sanhedrin** found Jesus guilty of **blasphemy** for claiming to be the Christ, the Son of God. He was then taken to Pontius Pilate, who found him innocent and offered to release either Jesus or the Jewish freedom fighter Barabbas. The crowd chose Barabbas and Jesus was condemned to death by crucifixion.

The crucifixion

The Gospels agree that Jesus was crucified on Friday, Simon of Cyrene carried the cross, a robber was crucified on either side of him, Jesus was mocked by the bystanders, Jesus forgave his killers and died with the words, 'Father into your hands I commend my spirit.'

The resurrection and ascension

Joseph of Arimathea was given permission to bury Jesus in his tomb and on Sunday morning Jesus' women followers came to anoint the body, found the tomb empty and told the disciples. Jesus then appeared to two disciples walking from Jerusalem to the village of Emmaus. Jesus continued to appear in Jerusalem for 40 days. Then he told the disciples to wait in Jerusalem for the gift of the Holy Spirit and was taken up from them into a cloud.

Importance of these events

- The Last Supper is the basis of the Mass, the most important form of Christian worship.
- Christians believe the crucifixion brought forgiveness from sin.

The Catholic Church teaches that the Paschal mystery guarantees humanity's salvation from sin because:
- Jesus freely offered himself for our salvation
- this offering was symbolised by Jesus breaking the bread and saying, 'This is my body given for you'.
- Christ's resurrection promises resurrection for all who believe
- by his ascension, Jesus Christ precedes believers into heaven so that believers may live in the hope of one day being with him for ever.

Blasphemy Speaking in a sacrilegious way about God or sacred things.

Paschal Relating to Easter.

Paschal mystery The term the Church uses to refer to the death and resurrection of Jesus and their effects on salvation.

Redemptive efficacy The term the Church uses to refer to the death and resurrection of Jesus guaranteeing humanity's salvation.

Sanhedrin The supreme religious authority in Israel in biblical times.

Sources of wisdom and authority

Luke's Gospel chapter 22 says that at the Last Supper, Jesus said the bread was his body and the wine was his blood.

Luke's Gospel chapter 23 says that when he was on the cross, Jesus asked God to forgive those crucifying him.

The Catechism teaches that the resurrection gives definite proof of Jesus' divine authority.

The Catechism teaches that the Paschal mystery is that by his death, Christ liberates us from sin; by his resurrection, he opens the way to a new life.

Now test yourself

1 Speaking in a sacrilegious way about God or sacred things is called:
   (a) Blasphemy
   (b) Paschal
   (c) Redemptive efficacy
   (d) Sanhedrin

2 A word meaning relating to Easter is:
   (a) Blasphemy
   (b) Paschal
   (c) Redemptive efficacy
   (d) Sanhedrin

3 The term the Church uses to refer to the death and resurrection of Jesus guaranteeing humanity's salvation is:
   (a) Blasphemy
   (b) Paschal
   (c) Redemptive efficacy
   (d) Sanhedrin

4 The supreme religious authority in Israel in biblical times was the:
   (a) Blasphemy
   (b) Paschal
   (c) Redemptive efficacy
   (d) Sanhedrin

Activities

Complete the answers to these questions:

1 Outline **three** features of the Paschal mystery.

One feature is the Last Supper when Jesus instituted the Eucharist. Another feature is the crucifixion when Jesus died on the cross for our sins. A third feature is

is the resurrection when Jesus rose from the dead

2 Explain **two** reasons why the Paschal mystery is important for Catholics. In your answer you must refer to a source of wisdom and authority.

The Paschal mystery is important for Catholics because part of the mystery is the Last Supper, which is the basis of the Mass, an essential part of Catholic life and the most important form of Christian worship.

Another reason is because the crucifixion brought forgiveness from sin, and the resurrection assures Christians that there is life after death. As the Catechism teaches, the Paschal mystery is that

by his death, Christ liberates us from sin; by his resurrection, he opens the way to a new life.

Exam support

You might be asked to evaluate a statement such as: *'The resurrection was the most important event in the life of Jesus.'* This table might help answer such a question:

Arguments for	Arguments against
• The resurrection proves that Jesus was the Son of God. • The resurrection is the basis of Christian belief as St Paul said, 'If Christ has not been raised, our preaching is useless and so is your faith.' • The resurrection of Jesus is the basis of the Christian belief in life after death and the promise that death is not the end. • The resurrection guarantees eternal life to Christians.	• The crucifixion is as important because it brought the forgiveness of sins without which Christians cannot get to heaven. • The Sermon on the Mount is as important because it records Jesus' teachings, which Christians need in order to know how to live their lives. • The Incarnation is important because without God becoming flesh in Jesus there could have been no resurrection. • Without the Last Supper there would be no Mass and no Blessed Sacrament.

Topic 1.1.7 The nature of salvation and grace

Salvation means being saved from **sin**. There are two types of sin:
- **Original sin** is inherited from the actions of the first humans. The Church teaches that everyone is born with original sin, which is washed away at baptism.
- Personal sin (actions that break God's law) is the consequence of a person's own actions.

Sin makes it difficult to have a relationship with God because sin separates a person from God. The Catholic Church teaches that Jesus came to Earth in order to restore the relationship through the salvation brought by his death on the cross.

Catholics believe salvation is important because:
- without salvation there can be no real relationship with God
- without salvation a person's sins will prevent them from entering heaven
- salvation from sin was the whole purpose of Jesus coming to Earth and founding Christianity.

Grace means mercy that is undeserved: Christ died for humanity's sins without humans doing anything to deserve it. By baptism a Christian receives the grace of Christ. The Holy Spirit then breathes love and strength (grace) into them, helping them work for the salvation of others. There are:
- sacramental graces which come from the sacraments
- special graces (**charisms**), such as the gift of healing, etc.
- the graces that come from special callings such as priests.

The Church teaches that Christians are given different gifts of grace and should use them according to the grace given to them.

Biblical teachings on salvation and grace

John's Gospel says that Jesus' mission was to bring God's salvation, 'For God so loved the world that he gave his one and only Son, that whoever believes in him shall not perish but have eternal life', and that this salvation gave the grace to live a Christian life.

The Acts of the Apostles say that St Peter preached that salvation comes through Jesus alone and this belief is backed up in the letters of Paul.

Evangelical Protestants, and some Catholics, agree that anyone who does not confess faith in Jesus cannot possibly be saved, but the Catholic Church teaches that no one but God knows who will and who will not be saved.

Implications for Catholic practice today

The Catholic Church teaches that grace comes through:
- receiving the sacraments of baptism and confirmation
- receiving the sacrament of reconciliation/confession
- receiving the sacrament of the Eucharist in the Mass
- leading a Christian life.

This means that the Catholic practices of encouraging families to have their children baptised, encouraging young adults to be confirmed, providing opportunities to receive the sacrament of reconciliation weekly, celebrating the Mass regularly and offering the weekly Mass on Sundays are tremendously important because they enable Catholics to maintain the grace and salvation necessary to enter heaven.

Charisms Special gifts or callings.

Grace Undeserved mercy from God which gives the strength to be good and holy.

Original sin The sin all humans are born with, which is washed away at baptism, though its effects, such as a mortal nature and selfish will, remain.

Salvation The act of delivering from sin or saving from evil, of healing a broken relationship with God.

Sin An act that is against God's will.

Sources of wisdom and authority

John's Gospel chapter 3 says, 'For God so loved the world that he gave his one and only Son, that whoever believes in him shall not perish but have eternal life.'

The Acts of the Apostles chapter 4 says that St Peter preached that salvation comes through Jesus alone.

The Catholic Catechism teaches that no one but God knows who will and who will not be saved.

Now test yourself

1 Charisms are:
   (a) special gifts or callings
   (b) bringing together people who were opposed to each other
   (c) the act of delivering from sin or saving from evil
   (d) an act that is against God's will

2 Grace is:
   (a) undeserved mercy from God which gives the strength to be good and holy
   (b) the act of delivering from sin or saving from evil
   (c) an act that is against God's will
   (d) reconciliation between God and humans

3 Salvation is:
   (a) reconciliation between God and humans
   (b) bringing together people who were opposed to each other
   (c) the act of delivering from sin or saving from evil
   (d) an act that is against God's will

4 Sin is:
   (a) reconciliation between God and humans
   (b) firm belief without logical proof
   (c) bringing together people who were opposed to each other
   (d) an act that is against God's will

Activities

Complete the answer to this question:

1 Explain **two** reasons why salvation is important for Catholics. In your answer you must refer to a source of wisdom and authority.

The Catholic Church believes that Jesus came to Earth in order to restore the relationship through the salvation brought by his death on the cross. 'Salvation' comes from the Latin 'salve', to heal. Jesus healed a broken relationship between humanity and God.

Catholics believe salvation is important because sin makes it difficult to have a relationship with God — sin separates a person from God and so without salvation there can be no real relationship with God.

Catholics also believe that without salvation a person's sins will prevent them from entering heaven, as John's Gospel says,

....

Exam support

You might be asked to evaluate a statement such as: *'Only those who have been saved from sin will get to heaven.'* This table might help answer such a question:

Arguments for	Arguments against
• The Church's teaching is that without salvation there can be no forgiveness of sins and so no entry to heaven. • St Peter said that salvation can only be found in Jesus and without Jesus there can be no salvation and so no entry to heaven. • John's Gospel teaches that those who do not believe in God's Son will perish, but those who do believe will have eternal life.	• The Church teaches that no one knows who will get to heaven. • Jesus said in the Sermon on the Mount that only those who do God's will get to heaven. • Jesus said in the Parable of the Sheep and the Goats that only those who help the hungry and homeless, etc. will enter heaven.

Eschatology refers to religious beliefs about death, judgement and life after death.

The Church teaches in the Catechism that:
- when people die, they are judged by God
- Christians who are perfectly purified will go to **heaven**
- Christians who have died with unforgiven sins (and possibly members of other religions and non-believers who have lived good lives) will go to **purgatory** to be purified
- very evil people who have totally rejected God will go to **hell**
- Christ will return at the end of the world when the dead will be raised, God will judge everyone and make a new heaven and a new Earth
- those purified in purgatory will go to heaven.

Catholics believe that heaven is perfection and eternal peace with God, which is, as the Catechism says, 'beyond human understanding and description'.

The Church believes in hell. God wishes for everyone to enter heaven, but people have to use their free will to achieve this.

The Bible is full of teachings about eschatology:
- John's Gospel records how Jesus raised Lazarus from the dead.
- St Paul says in his letters that Jesus' **resurrection** is a guarantee of life after death for Christians; everyone will be raised on the Last Day for a final judgement when the good will be rewarded in heaven, and the evil will go to hell.

Different Christian beliefs about life after death

- Non-Catholic Christians do not believe in purgatory because it is based on the teaching of the Church rather than the Bible.
- Some Evangelical Protestant Christians believe that when people die, their soul remains in the grave until the Last Day and a final judgement when born-again Christians will go to heaven and everyone else will go to hell.
- Most Liberal Protestants believe when the body dies, the soul leaves the body to live with God in a spirit world. Their belief in the **immortality of the soul** is based on the fact that after his ascension, Jesus became a spirit and went to the spirit world.

Why belief in life after death is important for Catholics

Belief in life after death is important for Catholics today because:
- they believe they will be judged by God so belief in life after death gives them an incentive to live a good Christian life by loving God and loving their neighbour
- they believe that sin can prevent people from going to heaven so they will try to avoid committing sins
- those beliefs give their lives meaning and purpose
- trying to love your neighbour as yourself is bound to affect a Catholic's life and explains why Catholic charities such as CAFOD are so involved in helping those in need.

Eschatology Religious beliefs about death, judgement and life after death.

Heaven A place of infinite peace in the presence of God.

Hell A place of eternal separation from the love of God.

Immortality of the soul The idea that the soul lives on after the death of the body.

Purgatory A preparation for heaven, a place of purification and healing.

Resurrection A belief that the body will be raised again to life but in a new, spiritual, transformed way.

Sources of wisdom and authority

Jesus said in John's Gospel chapter 11, 'I am the resurrection and the life', and that anyone who believes in him will not die.

St Paul said in Corinthians that the resurrection of Jesus was proved by many witnesses and guarantees eternal life for Christians.

The Catechism teaches that those who sincerely seek God but are not Catholic may gain eternal life.

Now test yourself

1 Beliefs about life after death are known as:
   (a) Eschatology
   (b) Immortality of the soul
   (c) Purgatory
   (d) Resurrection
2 The belief that at death the body dies but the soul lives on in a spiritual world is known as:
   (a) Eschatology
   (b) Immortality of the soul
   (c) Purgatory
   (d) Resurrection

3 The belief that after death the body stays in the grave until the end of the world, when it is raised, is known as:
   (a) Eschatology
   (b) Immortality of the soul
   (c) Purgatory
   (d) Resurrection
4 The place where Catholics believe souls go after death to be purified is called:
   (a) Eschatology
   (b) Immortality of the soul
   (c) Purgatory
   (d) Resurrection

Activities

Complete the answers to these questions:

1 Outline **three** features of Catholic teaching about life after death.

The Catholic Church teaches that after death the perfectly purified go to heaven. After death, evil people go to hell. Catholics with unforgiven sins

....

2 Explain **two** different Christian beliefs about life after death. In your answer you must refer to a source of wisdom and authority.

Some Evangelical Protestant Christians believe that when people die, their soul remains in the grave until the Last Day, when everyone will be judged by God. Those Christians who have been born again will go to heaven; everyone else will go to hell. This is based on Paul's teachings in 1 Corinthians 15.

Most Liberal Protestants believe that

....

....

Exam support

You might be asked to evaluate a statement such as: *'When you're dead, you're dead and that's the end of you.'* This table might help with such a question:

Arguments for	Arguments against
• Most beliefs in life after death assume that the mind or soul can survive in a non-material state without the body, but scientific evidence is that the human mind is totally dependent on the physical brain.	• The Bible record of the resurrection can be relied on because it is the Word of God.
• There is a problem as to where life after death could take place. Space exploration has shown there is no heaven above the sky and physics has shown there is no non-material world on Earth.	• The disciples must have known whether or not the resurrection happened and they would not have risked their lives as they did for something they knew was a lie.
• Life after death depends on there being a God, so people who do not believe in God have no reason to believe in life after death.	• The Church teaches the truth of life after death.
• If there is a non-material afterlife, how would we recognise souls without bodies? If souls survive death, they would be alone, with no way of contacting other souls.	• The arguments of philosophers such as Descartes show that the mind is separate from the body and so could survive without the body.
	• Heaven is a spiritual dimension, outside but interacting with the material universe.

1.2 Practices

Topic 1.2.1 The sacramental nature of reality

Christians believe that the whole of God's creation shows the presence of God in what Catholics call the sacramental nature of reality – God's power and nature can be understood and seen through the things he has made.

The Church's sacraments

Sacraments are outward signs that an inward gift of **grace** has been given by God. The Catholic Church celebrates seven **sacraments**.

The sacrament of baptism

- Practice – parents and godparents bring the child to church and the priest pours water over the child, baptising in the name of the Trinity, anoints with **chrism** and gives a lighted candle.
- Symbolism – the water symbolises washing away sin; the oil and candle symbolise being claimed by Christ.
- Meaning – the original sin with which the child is born is washed away.

Baptism is important for Catholics because:
- the Catechism teaches that without baptism, a person cannot receive the other sacraments
- baptism makes a person a full member of the Church, ready to begin a new life in the Holy Spirit
- baptism washes away original sin so that the baptised can achieve salvation and enter heaven.

The sacrament of confirmation

- Practice – the candidate renews the vows made on their behalf at baptism and the bishop lays his hands on the candidate and anoints them with chrism.
- Symbolism – the laying on of hands symbolises the gift of the Holy Spirit and the oil symbolises being called for a special task.
- Meaning – the confirmed person has fully joined the Catholic Church.

Confirmation is important because:
- it makes the person a full member of the Church
- only those who are confirmed can take on **lay ministries**
- it gives the strength of the Spirit to live the Christian life
- in baptism, promises were made by the person's parents and godparents, while in confirmation it is the individual's own choice to declare his or her belief.

The sacrament of the Eucharist

This sacrament is covered in detail in the next topic.

These three sacraments are known as sacraments of initiation because baptism cleanses original sin and brings a person into the Church, confirmation makes a person a full member of the Church, and the sacrament of the Eucharist unites them with Christ.

Chrism The oil used in baptism, confirmation and ordination.

Grace Undeserved blessing from God.

Lay ministries Special ways of serving the Church open to the non-ordained.

Sacraments Outward signs that an inward gift of grace has been given by God.

Sources of wisdom and authority

Catechism 300 teaches that 'God transcends creation and is present to it.'

Canon law says that the sacraments of baptism, confirmation and the Eucharist are required for full Christian initiation.

The Catechism says that confirmation binds a person perfectly to the Church and enriches with the gift of the Holy Spirit.

Now test yourself

1 Chrism is:
   (a) outward signs that an inward gift of grace has been given by God
   (b) the oil used in baptism, confirmation and ordination
   (c) undeserved blessing from God
   (d) special ways of serving the Church open to the non-ordained

2 Grace is:
   (a) outward signs that an inward gift of grace has been given by God
   (b) the oil used in baptism, confirmation and ordination
   (c) undeserved blessing from God
   (d) special ways of serving the Church open to the non-ordained

3 Lay ministries are:
   (a) outward signs that an inward gift of grace has been given by God
   (b) the oil used in baptism, confirmation and ordination
   (c) undeserved blessing from God
   (d) special ways of serving the Church open to the non-ordained

4 Sacraments are:
   (a) outward signs that an inward gift of grace has been given by God
   (b) the oil used in baptism, confirmation and ordination
   (c) undeserved blessing from God
   (d) special ways of serving the Church open to the non-ordained

Activities

Complete the answer to this question:

1 Explain **two** reasons why Catholics believe in the sacramental nature of reality. In your answer you must refer to a source of wisdom and authority.

Catholics believe in the sacramental nature of reality because they believe that God created the universe and everything in it — as shown in Genesis chapter 1. Therefore the whole of God's creation shows his presence and reveals his nature.

Another reason is that St Paul taught,

....

....

Exam support

You might be asked to evaluate a statement such as: *'Baptism is the most important sacrament.'* This table might help answer such a question:

Arguments for	Arguments against
• The Catechism teaches that baptism is the basis of the Christian life and without it, a person cannot receive the other sacraments. • Through baptism a person becomes a full member of the Church and is helped by the Church to begin a new life in the Holy Spirit and grow in faith. • Baptism washes away original sin so that the baptised can achieve salvation. • The Catechism says that baptism is necessary for salvation, and without salvation one cannot enter heaven.	• Holy orders are more important because without priests there can be no sacraments. • The Mass is more important because it brings Christ into the lives of Catholics at least once a week. • Reconciliation is more important because it forgives the sins you commit after baptism.

Topic 1.2.1 The sacramental nature of reality (continued)

The sacrament of reconciliation

The sacrament of reconciliation forgives a person's sins and brings them into a closer relationship with God. The penitent confesses their sins, admits responsibility and resolves not to sin again (**contrition**). The priest gives a **penance** and **absolution** giving the grace to make it easier to live a Christian life and receive the Eucharist.

The sacrament of anointing of the sick

The sacrament of the anointing of the sick gives seriously ill people the strength to face serious illness and death. The priest lays his hands on the sick person, anoints them with the oil of the sick, prays for the person, absolves their sins and gives them Holy Communion (**viaticum**).

The sacrament is important because it gives grace, spiritual strength and healing, and allows the person's sins to be forgiven so they can enter heaven.

The sacrament of marriage

Catholic marriage is a sacrament involving God as well as the bride and groom. During a Catholic wedding there are Bible readings, prayers, a homily on marriage and an exchange of vows and rings. This is usually followed by Nuptial Mass.

These practices give grace and strength for a life-long relationship of love and faithfulness, for the procreation of children and the raising of a Christian family.

The sacrament of holy orders

Holy orders is the sacrament when men are consecrated into the ordained ministry. The bishop lays his hands upon each candidate and anoints their hands with chrism at a special Mass, giving them the grace, strength and authority to administer the sacraments.

All Catholics believe the first five sacraments are essential for salvation.

Different views of the sacraments

Most Protestants believe only baptism and the Eucharist are essential for salvation because they were instituted by Jesus.

Some Protestants, for example Quakers and the Salvation Army, have no sacraments because they believe rituals belong to the old law of the Old Testament and not the new law of Jesus.

Some Protestants, for example Baptists and Pentecostals, believe only adults can be baptised because only adult baptism is referred to in the Bible.

Contrition Sorrow for the sin committed and deciding not to commit the sin again.

Penance An action showing contrition.

Absolution The words and actions of a priest assuring the pardon of sins.

Viaticum Food for the journey to God (the host given at the sacrament of anointing).

Sources of wisdom and authority

The Catechism teaches the sacraments are efficacious signs of grace instituted by Christ and the first five are essential for salvation.

The Catechism teaches that the seven sacraments are the way the Holy Spirit spreads the grace of Christ throughout the Church.

The Catechism says the sacrament of holy orders is the way by which the Holy Spirit enables priests to act in the person of Christ the Head.

Now test yourself

1 The words and actions of a priest assuring the pardon of sins is called:
   (a) Ordination
   (b) Viaticum
   (c) Absolution
   (d) Contrition

2 The host given at the sacrament of anointing is:
   (a) Ordination
   (b) Viaticum
   (c) Absolution
   (d) Contrition

3 Sorrow for the sin committed and deciding not to commit the sin again is known as:
   (a) Ordination
   (b) Viaticum
   (c) Absolution
   (d) Contrition

4 Making someone a priest, bishop or deacon by the sacrament of holy orders is:
   (a) Ordination
   (b) Viaticum
   (c) Absolution
   (d) Contrition

Activities

Complete the answers to these questions:

1 Outline **three** Catholic beliefs about sacraments.

Catholics believe that sacraments are outward signs that an inner gift of grace has been given. They believe that Catholics need to participate in the sacraments to gain salvation. The sacraments of initiation are

....

....

2 Explain **two** reasons why the sacraments are important for Catholics. In your answer you must refer to a source of wisdom and authority.

The sacraments are important for Catholics because they strengthen people's faith. The Catechism says that the seven sacraments are the way the Holy Spirit spreads the grace of Christ throughout the Church.

They are also important because they bring Christians closer

....

....

Exam support

You might be asked to evaluate a statement such as: *'The sacraments make it easier to be a good Christian.'* This table might help answer such a question:

Arguments for	Arguments against
• Through sacraments Christians receive grace (blessings) from God. • Sacraments mark the journey of faith that Christians go through in life. • Sacraments make Christians stronger in their faith. • Sacraments bring Christians closer to God. • A sacrament is an outward and visible sign of an inward, spiritual grace.	• Jesus said the most important things were to love God and love your neighbour, for which you don't need sacraments. • Good Christians such as Quakers and the Salvation Army do not have sacraments. • Some people take the sacraments but are racists. • Some people take the sacraments but will not help the poor.

Topic 1.2.2 Catholic liturgical worship

Liturgical worship uses a service book with set prayers and rituals so that everything follows the same format. The worshippers can follow the service and join in certain parts as they read the prayers and responses. The Bible readings for a year are set out in a **lectionary**, which follows the **liturgical year**, beginning at Advent and on through Christmas, Lent and Easter so that congregations hear most of the Bible read and follow the main events of the Church's year.

The main liturgical worship is the Mass, which Catholics should attend on Sundays and holy days. There is a set structure:

The Introductory Rite makes Catholics aware that they are sinners and includes the **Penitential Rite**.

- **The Liturgy of the Word** contains Bible readings when all stand for the Gospel reading as it contains the words of Christ.
- **The Liturgy of the Eucharist is** when the bread and wine are brought to the altar to be offered to God. The Eucharistic Prayer then re-enacts the Last Supper and the bread and wine are changed by **transubstantiation** into the body and blood of Christ. Catholics then receive Communion and the **hosts** consecrated at Mass but not given out during Communion, are reserved in the **tabernacle**.
- **The Concluding Rite** is when the people give thanks for what they have received and the congregation are given a blessing to help them in the week ahead.

The Mass is important and significant to Catholics because:

- the Eucharist is a sacrament which gives grace to live good lives and grow closer to God
- the Mass is a celebration of the resurrection, showing Catholics that there is eternal life
- Catholics are in the real presence of Christ and receive the body and blood of Christ, which joins them with Jesus, bringing them closer to salvation
- Jesus commanded attendance at Mass when he said at the Last Supper, 'Do this in memory of me.'

Different Christian understandings of liturgical worship

- Liturgical worship is the main form of worship in Catholic, Orthodox and many Anglican Churches, but is used only for Holy Communion, baptism, marriage and funerals in **Nonconformist** Churches.
- Nonconformist non-liturgical worship has:
  - hymns or gospel songs/choruses (accompanied by keyboards, etc. in more evangelical-type Churches)
  - extempore prayers (prayers without preparation, usually including thanksgiving, confession and intercession as in liturgical services)
  - emphasis on the sermon, relating the Bible readings to modern life.
- Catholics, Orthodox and Anglicans believe that liturgical worship allows the worshipper to think about the words and develop greater understanding and that the familiar rituals help them feel closer to God.
- **Nonconformists** believe non-liturgical worship allows worship to come from people's hearts and can be adapted to meet people's needs.

Hosts Sacramental unleavened bread.

Lectionary A list of Bible readings to be read at certain times of the year.

Liturgy A set form of public worship.

Liturgical year The Church's year from Advent to the Ordinary Sundays.

Nonconformists English Protestants who are not members of the Church of England.

Penitential Rite The confession and absolution at the beginning of the Mass.

Tabernacle A safe place in which the Blessed Sacrament is kept.

Transubstantiation The belief that during the Mass the bread and wine become the body and blood of Jesus through the power of the Holy Spirit.

Sources of wisdom and authority

The Catechism teaches that it is a sin knowingly to miss Sunday Mass and Mass on holy days of obligation.

The Catechism teaches that the Eucharist is the source and summit of the Christian life.

Lumen Gentium says that 'through taking the consecrated host we become one with Christ and are united with each other'.

Now test yourself

1 Sacramental unleavened bread is known as:
   (a) Tabernacle
   (b) Hosts
   (c) Transubstantiation
   (d) Lectionary

2 The list of Bible readings to be read at certain times of the year is called:
   (a) Tabernacle
   (b) Hosts
   (c) Transubstantiation
   (d) Lectionary

3 A safe place in which the Blessed Sacrament is kept is known as:
   (a) Tabernacle
   (b) Hosts
   (c) Transubstantiation
   (d) Lectionary

4 The belief that during the Mass the bread and wine become the body and blood of Jesus through the power of the Holy Spirit is called:
   (a) Tabernacle
   (b) Hosts
   (c) Transubstantiation
   (d) Lectionary

Activities

Complete the answers to these questions:

1 Outline **three** features of the Mass.

One feature is the Liturgy of the Word which is the Bible readings. A second feature is the Liturgy of the Eucharist when the bread and wine are offered, consecrated and shared with the people. A third feature is

....

....

2 Explain **two** reasons why there are different attitudes to liturgical worship among Christians. In your answer you must refer to a source of wisdom and authority.

Catholics, Orthodox and Anglicans believe that liturgical worship allows the worshipper to think about the words and develop greater understanding and the familiar rituals help them feel closer to God. Also, for Catholics, the Catechism says that the Eucharist is the source and summit of the Christian life.

Nonconformists believe

....

....

Exam support

You might be asked to evaluate a statement such as: *'Sunday Mass is the most important celebration a Catholic can take part in.'* This table might help answer such a question:

Arguments for	Arguments against
● The Mass is a sacrament which gives the grace Catholics need to live good lives and grow closer to God. ● The Mass is a celebration of the resurrection showing Catholics that there is eternal life. ● Catholics attend Mass to be in the real presence of Christ and receive the body and blood of Christ, which joins them with Jesus, bringing them closer to salvation. ● Jesus commanded attendance at Mass when he said at the Last Supper, 'Do this in memory of me.'	● Baptism is more important because without being baptised you cannot go to Mass. ● Marriage could be more important because without marriage there can be no children and humanity would come to an end. ● Easter celebrations are more important because without Easter there would be no Mass. ● Christmas celebration is more important because without Jesus coming to Earth there would be no Mass.

Topic 1.2.3 The Catholic funeral rite

The Catholic funeral rite involves the following:

- **A vigil service** may take place the night before the funeral in the church (or sometimes the family home or funeral home), This takes the form of a Service of the Word, a **eulogy** remembering the life of the deceased and prayers commending him/her to God. Many families take the body to stay in the church overnight.
- **The funeral liturgy** (preferably a Requiem Mass) is when the Church gathers with the family and friends of the deceased to give praise and thanks to God for Christ's victory over sin and death, and to commend the deceased to God's tender mercy and compassion. Prayers for pardon are said after the Mass and before burial (the absolution). They ask God that the person's soul will not have to suffer punishment in purgatory and will have requiem aeternam (eternal rest). The priest incenses the coffin and sprinkles it with holy water.
- **The Rite of Committal** takes place at the cemetery when there are scripture readings about resurrection, prayers of farewell and commendation. The coffin is sprinkled with holy water and lowered into the ground with a prayer for the eternal rest of the departed's soul and then the priest blesses the mourners.

Committal The burial of a dead body.

Eulogy A speech in praise of a dead person.

Requiem Mass The funeral Mass.

Vigil A period of devotional staying awake on the eve of a religious festival/funeral.

The aims of the funeral rite

The nature of the Requiem Mass allows for communion with the deceased. As the Catechism says, 'by the Requiem Mass, the family of the deceased learn to live in communion with the one who has fallen asleep in the Lord'.

The rite of committal shows the communion that exists between the Church on Earth and the Church in heaven: the deceased passes with the farewell prayers of the community of believers into the welcoming company of those who see God face to face.

The funeral rite in the home, the **Requiem Mass** and the **committal** all proclaim the Church's belief that Christians will share in Christ's eternal life.

The importance of the funeral rite

The funeral rite is important for Catholics because it:

- reminds them of the Church's faith that the Paschal mystery means that Catholic Christians will have eternal life
- proclaims the message of eternal life to the community
- assures the mourners that the deceased is still in the communion of the Church and will be reunited with loved ones at the end
- gives people a chance to celebrate the deceased's life.

The Mass at the funeral makes present the sacrifice of Christ so that the deceased's soul can be united with Christ himself.

Sources of wisdom and authority

The Catechism says that 'by the Requiem Mass, the family of the deceased learn to live in communion with the one who has fallen asleep in the Lord'.

Cardinal Vincent Nichols said that the Requiem Mass is the highest form of prayer, commending the soul of the deceased to God in union with Christ.

Now test yourself

1 Requiem aeternam means:
   (a) The burial of a dead body
   (b) A speech in praise of a dead person
   (c) A period of devotional staying awake
   (d) Eternal rest

2 Committal is:
   (a) The burial of a dead body
   (b) A speech in praise of a dead person
   (c) A period of devotional staying awake
   (d) Eternal rest

3 Eulogy is:
   (a) The burial of a dead body
   (b) A speech in praise of a dead person
   (c) A period of devotional staying awake
   (d) Eternal rest

4 Which of the following does not appear in the rite of committal?
   (a) Scripture readings about the resurrection
   (b) A speech in praise of a dead person
   (c) Sprinkling the coffin with holy water
   (d) Prayers of farewell

Activities

Complete the answers to these questions:

1 Outline **three** features of the Catholic funeral rite.

One feature is the vigil service the night before the funeral. Another feature is the Requiem Mass. A third feature is

....

....

2 Explain **two** reasons why the funeral rite is important for Catholics. In your answer you must refer to a source of wisdom and authority.

The funeral rite is important for Catholics because the nature of the Requiem Mass allows there to be communion with the deceased. As the Catechism says, 'by the Requiem Mass, the family of the deceased learn to live in communion with the one who has fallen asleep in the Lord'.

Another reason is that the rite of committal shows

....

....

....

Exam support

You might be asked to evaluate a statement such as: *'Church funerals help Catholics come to terms with death.'* This table might help answer such a question:

Arguments for	Arguments against
• A church funeral helps the family of the deceased to learn to live in communion with the one who has fallen asleep in the Lord. • Church funerals assure the mourners that the deceased is not gone, they are still in the communion of the Church and the mourners will be reunited with them at the end. • They give the mourners a chance to celebrate the life of the deceased. • The funeral rite in the home, the Requiem Mass and the committal all reassure the family that they will share in Christ's eternal life.	• Catholics whose faith is not strong may not be able to believe what is being said in the funeral rite. • Some may want to know why their loved one has been taken and the explanation that it is God's will may not be sufficient to help them. • Sometimes the loss of a loved one can cause such great grief that nothing can help.

Topic 1.2.4 Prayer

The main purpose of prayer is attempting to contact God, usually through words. However, prayer can also include **meditation** (thinking about religious matters) and **contemplation** (communion with God).

Prayer usually involves:
- **adoration**
- thanksgiving
- confession
- **supplication**, also called **intercession**.

Prayers can be **set prayers**, as used in liturgical worship, and learned prayers, such as the Hail Mary, Come Holy Spirit, Hail Holy Queen, or **informal prayers** to express innermost thoughts to God using your own words, to bring a more personal relationship with God.

Most Catholics will use the Our Father (Lord's Prayer) a lot in their personal contacts with God because this is how Jesus told them to pray in Matthew's Gospel. It expresses:
- adoration (hallowed be your name, your kingdom come, your will be done on Earth as it is in heaven)
- **confession** (forgive us our debts, as we also have forgiven our debtors)
- supplication (give us today our daily bread … and lead us not into temptation, but deliver us from the evil one).

When Catholics pray

Catholics pray in public worship, in informal worship with groups of Christians, when they wake up or before they go to bed, or at any moment when the thought of God enters their mind. Many Catholics pray at set times each day.

Why Christians pray (and the importance of prayer)

Catholics pray because:
- they want a relationship with God
- Jesus said Christians should pray
- the Catechism says Christians should pray
- contemplative and meditative prayers can bring inner peace
- their prayer life helps them to have a healthy emotional life.

Why it is important to have a variety of types of worship

Worship is tremendously important for Catholics because Jesus said that the greatest commandment is to worship God with all your heart and all your soul, and this requires people to be able to worship in a variety of ways:
- Worship in the home – because this is the heart of people's lives and worshipping as a family brings the family together.
- Private worship – to communicate with God one to one and express private emotions a person cannot express in front of others.
- Public worship – worshipping with others in church, especially at Mass, gives a sense of belonging to a whole community of believers.
- Worship at set times – gives order and purpose to people's religious life and means worship is never forgotten.
- Joyful worship – worship needs to be able to reflect people's moods.
- Serious worship – people need to worship God when they are thinking about the meaning of life, such as during Lent and at sad times like death.

Adoration Praising or adoring God for what he is.

Confession Prayers saying sorry for sins and asking God's forgiveness.

Contemplation Communion with God.

Meditation Thinking about religious matters.

Supplication/intercession Prayers asking for God's help.

Sources of wisdom and authority

Jesus said that the greatest commandment is to love God with all your heart and with all your soul and with all your mind and with all your strength.

In Matthew's Gospel, Jesus taught his followers the Our Father as the best way to pray.

The Catechism says that prayer 'is the raising of one's heart and mind to God.'

Now test yourself and Activities answers at **www.hoddereducation.co.uk/myrevisionnotes**

Now test yourself

1 Prayers praising God for what he is are called:
   (a) Adoration
   (b) Contemplation
   (c) Meditation
   (d) Supplication

2 Prayers bringing communion with God are called:
   (a) Adoration
   (b) Contemplation
   (c) Meditation
   (d) Supplication

3 Prayer silently thinking about religious matters is called:
   (a) Adoration
   (b) Contemplation
   (c) Meditation
   (d) Supplication

4 Prayers asking for God's help are called:
   (a) Adoration
   (b) Contemplation
   (c) Meditation
   (d) Supplication

Activities

Complete the answers to these questions:

1 Outline **three** features of prayer.

One feature is adoration, praising God for what he is. Another feature is thanksgiving, thanking God for the good things of life. A third feature is

....

....

2 Explain **two** reasons why it is important for Catholics to have different forms of worship. In your answer you must refer to a source of wisdom and authority.

Worship is tremendously important for Catholics because Jesus said that the greatest commandment is to worship God with all your heart and all your soul, which requires people to be able to worship in a variety of ways. For example, worship in the home is needed because the home is the heart of the family and worshipping as a family brings the family together.

Catholics also need public worship because

....

....

....

Exam support

You might be asked to evaluate a statement such as: *'Praying helps make you a better person.'* This table might help answer such a question:

Arguments for	Arguments against
• The Gospels show that Jesus prayed a lot and he was a perfect person. • The saints of the Church all prayed a lot and they were extremely good people. • Prayer brings you close to God and the closer you get to God, the better person you will become. • Prayer, especially prayers of supplication, give God's help and strength, which are needed to become a better person.	• Prayer is only about feelings, but it is actions that make you a better person. • Not all people who pray become better; some people who pray a lot are quite nasty people. • Prayer is mainly about your relationship with God, but being a better person is about your relationships with other people.

Topic 1.2.5 Forms of popular piety

Popular piety refers to the forms of prayer and worship which come from people's responses to the Church's liturgy.

The Rosary

The Rosary is a set of prayers based on the Joyful Mysteries (the early days of Jesus), the Luminous Mysteries (from Jesus' baptism to the Last Supper), the Sorrowful Mysteries (the betrayal, trials and crucifixion) and the Glorious Mysteries (the resurrection, ascension, assumption of the Blessed Virgin).

Praying the Rosary:
- reminds Catholics of the life of Christ
- reminds Catholics of what Christ has done for them
- brings spiritual gifts such as humility, love of neighbour and true wisdom
- brings comfort and identity as a Catholic.

Eucharistic adoration

Eucharistic adoration is adoration focused on the Blessed Sacrament. It may be performed when the Eucharist is exposed for viewing, displayed in a **monstrance** on an altar with a light focused on it, or with candles. Adoration often takes place when the Eucharist is not exposed but left in a **ciborium** on the altar or in the **tabernacle**. Many Catholics perform Eucharistic adoration for an uninterrupted hour known as the **holy hour.**

Eucharistic adoration:
- helps the worshipper to make contact with the presence of Christ
- is a way of honouring and adoring Christ
- helps to cancel out the world's evils and bring world peace
- follows the example of the Popes.

The Stations of the Cross

The Stations of the Cross are 14 images depicting the journey of Jesus on Good Friday from his sentencing to his body being put in the tomb. The images are arranged in order around a church so that worshippers can stop at each station to say set prayers or simply to meditate on what happened. The celebration of the Stations mainly happens on the Fridays of Lent, especially Good Friday.

Catholics celebrate the Stations because it helps them:
- identify with the sufferings of Jesus
- pray through the journey of Jesus to the cross
- remember the cost of the salvation Jesus brought
- give thanks for what Jesus did for them.

The Church believes that popular piety is a good way for Catholics to express their devotion as long as they are in accord with Church teachings.

Different Christian attitudes

Protestant Christians do not:
- pray the Rosary because they will not have anything to do with adoration of the Virgin Mary – they believe she was an ordinary woman and do not accept the assumption or immaculate conception
- practise Eucharistic adoration because they do not believe in transubstantiation
- follow the Stations of the Cross because they are not all based on the Bible.

Ciborium A receptacle for the Blessed Sacrament.

Holy hour An hour spent in Eucharistic adoration.

Monstrance The vessel used for the exhibition of the Blessed Sacrament.

A rosary The prayer beads used to help in praying the Rosary.

The Rosary The set series of prayers based on the rosary beads.

Tabernacle A safe place in which the Blessed Sacrament is kept.

Sources of wisdom and authority

The Catechism teaches that praying the Rosary is important because it helps Catholics to meditate on the work of Christ.

The Catechism teaches that adoration of the Blessed Sacrament stimulates the faithful to an awareness of the marvellous presence of Christ and encourages spiritual communion with Him.

St Dominic was promised that praying the Rosary gives Mary's special protection against evil and heresy.

Now test yourself

1 A receptacle for the Blessed Sacrament is called:
- (a) The Rosary
- (b) A rosary
- (c) A ciborium
- (d) A tabernacle

2 The prayer beads used to help in praying are known as:
- (a) The Rosary
- (b) A rosary
- (c) A ciborium
- (d) A tabernacle

3 The set series of prayers based on the rosary beads is called:
- (a) The Rosary
- (b) A rosary
- (c) A ciborium
- (d) A tabernacle

4 A safe place in which the Blessed Sacrament is kept is:
- (a) The Rosary
- (b) A rosary
- (c) A ciborium
- (d) A tabernacle

Activities

Complete the answers to these questions:

1 Outline **three** forms of popular piety.

One form of popular piety is praying the Rosary using rosary beads. Another form of popular piety is Eucharistic adoration, which is when someone adores the blessed sacrament. A third form of popular piety is

....

....

2 Give **two** reasons why Eucharistic adoration is important for Catholics. In your answer you must refer to a source of wisdom and authority.

Eucharistic adoration is important because adoring the real presence of Christ in the consecrated hosts helps the worshipper to make contact with the presence of Christ. The Catechism teaches that adoration of the Blessed Sacrament stimulates the faithful to an awareness of the marvellous presence of Christ and encourages spiritual communion with Him.

Another reason is

....

....

....

Exam support

You might be asked to evaluate a statement such as: *'You can gain more from contemplation and reflection than from liturgical worship.'* This table might help answer such a question:

Arguments for	Arguments against
Contemplation such as: ● Eucharistic adoration helps the worshipper to make contact with the presence of Christ ● the holy hour helps to cancel out the evils of the world and bring world peace ● praying the Rosary brings spiritual gifts (fruits of the mystery), such as humility, love of neighbour and true wisdom ● the Stations of the Cross helps Catholics identify with the sufferings of Jesus and remember the cost of salvation.	Liturgical worship: ● gives the grace Catholics need to live good lives and grow closer to God ● is a celebration of the resurrection, showing Catholics that there is eternal life ● allows Catholics to receive the body and blood of Christ, which joins them with Jesus, bringing them closer to salvation ● brings Catholics into communion with their fellow members of Christ's Body.

Topic 1.2.6 Pilgrimage

The nature, history and purpose of Catholic pilgrimage

Christians have been going on pilgrimage since the early days of Christianity. Pilgrimage to the Holy Land and to places connected with the saints and to **venerate** their **relics** were made to gain God's forgiveness for sins or for healing from illness.

Catholics go on pilgrimage:
- to become closer to God
- to add discipline to their spiritual life
- to be cured from illness or to gain inner strength to cope with illnesses
- so that some of the holiness from the great figures or events connected with pilgrimage sites will rub off.

Four great pilgrimage sites

Jerusalem is where the crucial events in the last week of Jesus' life took place. Christian pilgrims visit the **Cenacle**, the Church of All Nations on the Mount of Olives (where Jesus was arrested), the Convent of the Sisters of Zion (the site where Pilate tried Jesus), the **Via Dolorosa** and the Church of the Holy Sepulchre, which contains the tomb where Jesus was buried and rose from the dead.

Rome is a major place of pilgrimage for Catholics because it contains Vatican City (the headquarters of the Church and home of the Pope) and the four **papal basilicas**. St Peter's contains the tomb of St Peter and is where the Pope presides at liturgies throughout the year. St John Lateran contains the Holy Stairs (brought from Jerusalem), on which Jesus walked at his trial. St Paul outside the Walls is the burial place of St Paul. Santa Maria Maggiore which contains the Crypt of the Nativity with wood from Jesus' Holy Crib.

Lourdes has been a pilgrimage centre since St Bernadette witnessed the miraculous appearances of the Virgin Mary and was led to a grotto where a miraculous spring appeared. Since these events Lourdes has become a great place of pilgrimage for Catholics (6 million a year) and many healing miracles are alleged to have taken place there. There is a Eucharistic procession every afternoon, and the Rosary Procession in the evening.

Walsingham is the village in Norfolk where the Lady of the Manor had a vision of the Virgin Mary ordering her to build a copy of Mary's home in Nazareth. Modern pilgrims believe they can feel close to the Virgin Mary when praying there. There are claims of healings taking place there and it brings Catholics and Anglicans closer together.

Different Christian attitudes to pilgrimage

Protestant Christians feel that emphasising special 'holy places' is wrong because believers can encounter God anywhere – God is the same God everywhere. They oppose any form of worshipping the Virgin Mary and any veneration of saints and relics, so they visit the holy places in Jerusalem but not Rome, Lourdes or Walsingham.

Cenacle The Upper Room in Jerusalem where the Last Supper took place.

Papal basilica A title given to the four highest-ranking buildings of the Catholic Church.

Relic A part of a dead saint's body or belongings.

Venerate Treat with deep religious respect.

Via Dolorosa 'The way of tears', the route Jesus took from Pilate's court to Golgotha.

Sources of wisdom and authority

The Catechism teaches that 'pilgrimage can strengthen faith and increase knowledge of the mystery of Christ'.

Luke's Gospel records that Jesus went on pilgrimage: 'every year his parents went to Jerusalem for the Feast of the Passover.'

Now test yourself

1 The Cenacle is:
   (a) The Upper Room in Jerusalem where the Last Supper took place
   (b) Something promoting Christians' unity
   (c) Part of a dead saint's body or belongings
   (d) Being treated with deep religious respect
2 A relic is:
   (a) The Upper Room in Jerusalem where the Last Supper took place
   (b) Something promoting Christians' unity
   (c) Part of a dead saint's body or belongings
   (d) Being treated with deep religious respect

3 The title given to the four highest-ranking buildings of the Catholic Church is:
   (a) Papal bull
   (b) Papal minster
   (c) Papal basilica
   (d) Papal encyclical
4 Venerate means:
   (a) The Upper Room in Jerusalem where the Last Supper took place
   (b) Something promoting Christians' unity
   (c) Part of a dead saint's body or belongings
   (d) Treat with deep religious respect

Activities

Complete the answers to these questions:

1 Outline **three** places visited by pilgrims to Jerusalem.

Pilgrims visit the Cenacle, which is the site of the Upper Room. They visit the Via Dolorosa, which is the route Jesus took to his crucifixion. A third place they visit is

....

....

2 Explain **two** reasons why pilgrimage is important for Catholics. In your answer you must refer to a source of wisdom and authority.

One reason pilgrimage is important for Catholics is because pilgrims are following the example of Jesus. Luke's Gospel records that Jesus went on pilgrimage to Jerusalem every Passover.

Another reason is

....

....

....

Exam support

You might be asked to evaluate a statement such as: *'All Catholics should go on pilgrimage to Rome.'* This table might help answer such a question:

Arguments for	Arguments against
Rome contains: ● Vatican City, the headquarters of the Church and the home of the Pope ● the four papal basilicas, which are designated as pilgrim churches ● St Peter's, which has the tomb of St Peter below the high altar and the tombs of many Popes, and is where the Pope presides at liturgies throughout the year ● St Paul Outside the Walls, which is the burial place of St Paul.	● Many Christians have more important Christian duties to fulfil, such as helping the less fortunate. ● Christians bringing up a family should put their family's needs first. ● Pilgrimage is expensive and Christians should use their spare money to help the less fortunate, as Jesus showed in the Parable of the Sheep and the Goats. ● All the things people do on pilgrimage can be done by watching and meditating on a video.

Topic 1.2.7 Catholic social teaching

Catholic social teaching is based on:

- Jesus' command to love your neighbour as yourself
- the teaching of the Bible and the Catechism that God wants the world to be ruled justly, meaning people should be treated fairly and not cheated
- Jesus' teaching in the Parable of the Sheep and the Goats that Christians should help feed the hungry, visit the sick and those in prison, and shelter the homeless
- the teaching of St Paul and the Church that Christians should try to live in peace with everyone and be committed to forgiveness and love in order to bring about **reconciliation** and the ending of conflict
- the teaching of the Catechism that Catholics should practise the **cardinal virtues**
- the *Laudato Si* and *Evangelii Gaudium* **encyclicals** by Pope Francis, which urge Catholics to tackle environmental problems such as climate change and pollution, and the problems of world poverty
- the belief that Christians have a **vocation** to serve God and love their neighbour.

Christian vocation must involve everything a Christian does and many Catholics are led by the Church's social teachings to work for and/or support the work of SVP and CAFOD (see below).

St Vincent de Paul Society (SVP)

SVP helps to relieve poverty and suffering in the United Kingdom by organising:

- regular visiting and personal care for the lonely, bereaved, depressed and housebound
- diocesan children's camps for children from poor or broken homes
- furniture stores for unwanted furniture to use for the homeless
- housing associations to provide affordable housing for the homeless, overcrowded poor families, etc.
- drop-in centres for lonely people to have opportunities to socialise.

Catholic Fund for Overseas Development (CAFOD)

CAFOD tries to end world poverty through:

- promoting long-term development so that **LEDCs** can become self-supporting
- a disaster fund to deal with natural disasters and refugees, which often have to take priority over long-term aid (CAFOD has provided more than £2 million to support church partners in Syria)
- educating the people and Churches of England and Wales about the need for development and the ways in which Catholics can help less developed countries
- speaking out on behalf of poor communities to bring social justice, such as the Trade Justice Campaign
- promoting Fairtrade products to bring better prices, decent working conditions, local sustainability, and fair terms of trade for farmers and workers in the developing world.

Cardinal virtues The major virtues — justice, prudence, temperance and fortitude.

Encyclical A letter addressed by the Pope to all the bishops of the Church.

LEDC Less economically developed countries.

Reconciliation Bringing together people who were opposed to one another.

Vocation The calling a person has to live in a certain way.

Sources of wisdom and authority

Jesus said in Mark's Gospel that the greatest commandments are to love God with all your heart and soul and mind and strength and to love your neighbour as yourself.

St Paul said in Romans 14, 'Let us therefore make every effort to do what leads to peace and to mutual edification'.

Pope Francis said in Evangelii Gaudium that the world must listen to 'both the cry of the earth and the cry of the poor'.

Now test yourself

1 A letter addressed by the Pope to all the bishops of the Church is called:
   (a) Reconciliation
   (b) Vocation
   (c) Encyclical
   (d) Missive

2 Bringing together people who were opposed to one another is:
   (a) Reconciliation
   (b) Vocation
   (c) Encyclical
   (d) Missive

3 The calling a person has to live in a certain way is:
   (a) Reconciliation
   (b) Vocation
   (c) Encyclical
   (d) Missive

Activities

Complete the answers to these questions:

1 Outline **three** ways by which CAFOD tries to end world poverty.

CAFOD tries to end world poverty by promoting long-term development so that LEDCs can become self-supporting. Another way is by having a disaster fund to deal with natural disasters and refugees. A third way is by

....

....

2 Explain **two** reasons why Catholics support the work of the CAFOD. In your answer you must refer to a source of wisdom and authority.

Catholics support the work of CAFOD because they help the poor, the lonely, the bereaved and the depressed and so it is a way of loving your neighbour and Jesus said in Mark's Gospel that Christians should love their neighbour.

A second reason is that it is a way of responding to Pope Francis' encyclical, 'Laudato Si', which says that the world must listen to

....

....

....

Exam support

You might be asked to evaluate a statement such as: *'It is more important to save people's souls than feed their bodies.'* This table might help answer such a question:

Arguments for	Arguments against
• The Church's teaching is that without salvation there can be no forgiveness of sins and so no entry to heaven. • Without salvation there can be no real relationship with God. • Without salvation a person's sins are likely to condemn them to eternal hell. • Salvation from sin was the whole purpose of Jesus coming to Earth and founding Christianity.	• Jesus said that Christians should love their neighbours, which means feeding their bodies. • Jesus said in the Parable of the Sheep and the Goats that Christians should feed the hungry. • Justice is one of the cardinal Christian virtues and giving justice to the poor must mean feeding their bodies. • Pope Francis said in *Laudato Si* that Christians must listen to the cry of the poor.

Topic 1.2.8 Catholic mission and evangelisation

A missionary is a person sent by a Church into an area to bring people into the Christian Church. **Evangelisation** is proclaiming the message of Christianity with the aim of converting people to Christianity.

Jesus' final words to his disciples were to go and make disciples of all nations, known by Christians as 'the **Great Commission**', so it is something they must do.

The disciples began this work immediately. St Peter organised missions throughout Palestine, then St Philip converted an Ethiopian, leading to Christianity spreading into Africa. St Paul founded Christian Churches throughout the Eastern Mediterranean, St Peter founded the Church in Rome and St Thomas took Christianity to India. There were also Christian Churches in North Africa and Europe by 100CE.

When Europeans began to colonise America and Africa, Christian missionaries went with them so that conversion to Christianity went hand in hand with **colonisation**. South and Central America became Catholic through the work of Spanish and Portuguese Catholics, while North America and much of Africa south of the Sahara became Protestant through the work of British missionaries. (French and Belgian African colonies became Catholic.)

Alpha The Christian course trying to convert non-churchgoers.

Catechetical programmes Religious instruction given in preparation for Christian baptism or confirmation.

Colonisation Originally strong countries ruling weak countries, now it means rich countries treating poor countries as if they were colonies.

Evangelisation Seeking to convert to Christianity.

Great Commission Jesus' last command to his disciples to go out and convert the world.

Missionary and evangelical work

Missionary and evangelical work is carried out locally and globally:
- Local churches which celebrate the Mass offer the sacraments to the people, provide discussion and prayer groups, support the local Catholic Christian schools and provide social facilities, so bringing people into the Church.
- Churches Together in England, which co-ordinates the work of groups such as **Alpha**.
- The Pontifical Council for the promotion of New Evangelisation helps local bishops in teaching young people, families and those converting to Catholicism.
- The Society for the Propagation of the Faith is in charge of the mission dioceses of the Catholic Church and works with them to provide **catechetical programmes**, seminaries, churches, orphanages and schools.

Why missionary and evangelical work is important for Catholics

- Evangelising is the Great Commission of Jesus.
- Christians believe that being a Christian helps people to share God's love, gives strength to cope with life and assures people a place in heaven, therefore it should be shared with those outside the faith.
- Christianity in England has experienced a decline – attendance at Mass was 30 per cent lower in 2010 than in 1993.

Sources of wisdom and authority

Jesus' final instruction to his disciples in Matthew's Gospel was to go and make disciples of all nations, baptising them in the name of the Father and of the Son and of the Holy Spirit.

In *Evangelii Gaudium*, Pope Francis appealed for Catholics to become 'spirit-filled Evangelisers'.

Now test yourself

TESTED

1 The Christian course trying to convert non-churchgoers is called:
(a) Catechetical programmes
(b) The Great Commission
(c) Alpha
(d) Evangelisation

2 Religious instruction given in preparation for Christian baptism or confirmation is known as:
(a) Catechetical programmes
(b) The Great Commission
(c) Alpha
(d) Evangelisation

3 Seeking to convert to Christianity is known as:
(a) Catechetical programmes
(b) The Great Commission
(c) Alpha
(d) Evangelisation

4 Jesus' last command to his disciples to go out and convert the world was:
(a) Catechetical programmes
(b) The Great Commission
(c) Alpha
(d) Evangelisation

Activities

Complete the answers to these questions:
1 Outline **three** features of early Christian missions.

One feature is that St Peter organised missions throughout Palestine. A second feature is that St Philip converted an Ethiopian, leading to Christianity spreading into Africa. A third feature is

....

....

2 Explain **two** reasons why mission and evangelism are important for Catholics. In your answer you must refer to a source of wisdom and authority.

Mission and evangelism are important for Catholics because evangelising is the Great Commission of Jesus, given just before the ascension when Jesus told his disciples, in Matthew's Gospel, to go and make disciples of all nations, baptising them in the name of the Father and of the Son and of the Holy Spirit.

Another reason is

....

....

....

Exam support

You might be asked to evaluate a statement such as: *'There shouldn't be any missionaries in the modern world.'* This table might help answer such a question:

Arguments for	Arguments against
• Trying to convert followers of other religions can be seen as a type of prejudice and discrimination and can lead to violence. • Trying to convert people from another religion means thinking their religion is wrong, which would require study and comparison of all religions and a way of deciding which is true. • LEDCs can resent overseas missions as a new form of colonisation.	• Being missionaries is the Great Commission Jesus gave his disciples just before the ascension. • The two greatest saints of the Church, St Peter and St Paul, were missionaries. • Christians believe that being a Christian helps people to share God's love, gives strength to cope with life and assures people a place in heaven, therefore it should be shared with those outside the faith.

Topic 1.2.8 Catholic mission and evangelisation

1.3 Sources of wisdom and authority

Topic 1.3.1 The Bible

The word 'bible' means books and so the Bible is a library of books.

The terms Old and New Testament are Christian. Christians regard the Old Testament as God's old covenant (testament) which was fulfilled by the new covenant brought by Jesus. Jewish people call the books of the Old Testament the **Tenakh**, their holy book.

The Old Testament is divided into:
- the **Torah** – first five books of Moses containing all the laws of Judaism, including the **Decalogue**
- the Prophets – the history books, such as Joshua and Judges, and the books by prophets such as Isaiah and Jeremiah who believed they had a message from God to the people
- the Writings – poetry such as the Psalms, wise sayings such as Proverbs and **apocalyptic** writings such as Daniel.

The New Testament is divided into:
- Four Gospels of Matthew, Mark, Luke and John which record the life and teachings of Jesus Christ
- The Acts of the Apostles, which records the history of the early Church from the ascension to St Paul's arrival in Rome
- The Letters written by St Paul (14) St John (3), St Peter (2), St Jude and St James to encourage and instruct early groups of Christians
- Revelation, an apocalyptic, prophetic book about the last things.

Why the Bible is important for Catholics
- The Bible records the teaching of Jesus which shows Christians what to believe, how to live and how to make decisions.
- The Bible records the life, death and resurrection of Jesus, which is the basis of the Christian faith.
- The Bible contains the Decalogue, which are God's basic guidelines on how to live.
- The Bible reveals what God is like and what he does for Christians.

Different Christian understandings about which books should be in the Bible

In the early days of the Church there was no agreement as to which books were to make up the Bible.

The Churches did not finally agree on which books were to be in the New Testament until the Council of Carthage in 397. The Greek Old Testament (**Septuagint**) and The Carthage New Testament was accepted by Catholics and Orthodox Christians, and was the Bible translated into Latin by St Jerome (**Vulgate**), declared the Catholic Bible at the Council of Trent.

At the Reformation the Protestant scholars used the Hebrew Old Testament, so Protestant Bibles have 39 books in their Old Testament whereas Catholic and Orthodox Bibles have 47 books.

Apocalyptic Religious writing teaching spiritual truths about eschatology (death, judgement and the future life).

Decalogue The Ten Commandments.

Septuagint The Greek Old Testament.

Tenakh The Jewish Bible.

Torah The five books of Law in the Old Testament.

Vulgate The Latin Bible.

Sources of wisdom and authority

St Paul said in his second letter to Timothy that 'All scripture is inspired by God.'

The Catechism says that God is the author of Sacred Scripture and so the Bible teaches without error God's saving truth.

Now test yourself

1 The Jewish Bible is known as the:
   (a) Septuagint
   (b) Tenakh
   (c) Torah
   (d) Vulgate
2 The Greek Old Testament is known as the:
   (a) Septuagint
   (b) Tenakh
   (c) Torah
   (d) Vulgate
3 The five books of Law in the Old Testament are known as the:
   (a) Septuagint
   (b) Tenakh
   (c) Torah
   (d) Vulgate
4 The Latin Bible is known as the:
   (a) Septuagint
   (b) Tenakh
   (c) Torah
   (d) Vulgate

Activity

Complete the answers to these questions:
1 Outline **three** types of literature in the Old Testament.

The Old Testament contains the law books of the Torah. It also contains history and prophecy in the Prophet books like Isaiah and Jeremiah. It also has

....

2 Explain **two** reasons why the Bible is important for Catholics. In your answer you must refer to a source of wisdom and authority.

The Bible is important for Catholics because it reveals what God is like and what he does for Christians. The Catechism says that God is the author of Sacred Scripture and so the Bible teaches without error God's saving truth.

Another reason the Bible is important is because

....

....

....

Exam support

You might be asked to evaluate a statement such as: *'If the Bible came from God, all Christians would use the same Bible.'* This table might help answer such a question:

Arguments for	Arguments against
● If God sent the Bible, he would have made sure that all Christians received exactly the same Bible so there would be no arguments. ● If the Bible is God's words that God wanted humans to hear, he would have made sure everyone got the same words. ● God is all-powerful so there is nothing to stop him from preventing different versions of the Bible from appearing. ● The fact that the Catholic Bible is different from the Protestant Bible makes it easy for non-religious people to say that the Bible does not come from God.	● The differences are very small. There are only eight books in the Catholic Bible which are not in the Protestant Bible. ● Protestants accept that those eight books are useful for moral instruction, but not for doctrine. ● The Catechism says that God inspired the authors of the Bible, not that he controlled them, and it is to be expected that there would be some differences. ● The way Christians argued about which books should be in the Bible and had a slight disagreement about 8 of the 74 is a good reason for believing that the 66 can be relied on.

Catholics and the inspiration of the Bible

Catholics believe:
- the Bible is inspired by the Holy Spirit, which means it comes from God and gives the truth and should be accepted and followed by Catholics
- God speaks through the Bible, showing his character and commands, so it should be followed
- the Bible contains God's laws on how to behave, showing how God wants them to live, especially in the Gospels where Jesus teaches how to live the Christian life.

Catholics and the interpretation of the Bible

Catholics believe that the Bible is not always clear in its meaning. So although Catholics are encouraged to be inspired by the Bible through reading it alone using the **Lectio Divina** method used in monasteries, true Catholic interpretation of the Bible needs help from the Church, which is given by:
- the Apostolic Tradition
- the **magisterium** of the Church
- the **Catechism** of the Church
- papal encyclicals
- bishops' letters
- homilies by the priest.

Different interpretations of the authority of the Bible

- **Fundamentalist Christians believe** that the Bible is not only the Word of God but also the words of God. It is the literal word of God. They think the Bible was written by people who simply wrote down what God dictated to them. This means that every word in the Bible is the word of God and so is true.
- **Conservative Christians believe** that the Bible is the revealed word of God but not his actual words. This means they think the writers of the Bible were inspired by God and guided by God in what they wrote, but they used their own ideas. Conservatives see the Bible as a book about faith rather than a book about science.
- **Liberal Christians believe** that the Bible is words about God rather than the words of God. They feel that the Bible writers were people who had special insights or experiences of God which they wrote in their own way. This means there may well be mistakes and contradictions in the Bible, but what matters are the great truths about God that the Bible contains.

The Bible as a source of guidance and teaching

Catholics believe the Bible is a source of guidance and teaching because it:
- is inspired by the Holy Spirit, which means it comes from God and is therefore holy and authoritative because it gives God's truths
- reveals God – God speaks through both the Old Testament and the New Testament, showing his character and commands
- contains God's laws on how to behave, such as the Ten Commandments – these rules are there to help people live as God intends, so it gives guidance
- contains the teachings of Jesus on how to live the Christian life. Catholics believe Jesus is the second person of the Holy Trinity so what he taught has authority, which means that the Bible that records his teaching is a source of guidance.

Catechism The official teaching of the Catholic Church.

Conservative One who believes the Bible is the revealed word of God, not his actual words.

Fundamentalist One who believes the Bible is the literal or actual words of God.

Lectio Divina A way of studying passages from the Bible with prayer and meditation.

Liberal One who believes the Bible was written by humans inspired by God.

Magisterium The teaching office of the Church.

Sources of wisdom and authority

St Paul said in his second letter to Timothy, 'All scripture is inspired by God.'

The Catechism teaches that God inspired the human authors of the sacred books of scripture.

The Catechism teaches that since the authors were inspired by God and what they wrote has been affirmed by the Holy Spirit, so the books of the Bible teach the truth and are a source of guidance for the faithful.

Now test yourself

1 The official teaching of the Catholic Church is:
   (a) Liberal
   (b) Conservative
   (c) Catechism
   (d) Fundamentalist
2 One who believes the Bible is the revealed Word of God, not his actual words, is a:
   (a) Liberal
   (b) Conservative
   (c) Catechism
   (d) Fundamentalist
3 One who believes the Bible was written by humans inspired by God is a:
   (a) Liberal
   (b) Conservative
   (c) Catechism
   (d) Fundamentalist
4 One who believes the Bible is the actual words of God is a:
   (a) Liberal
   (b) Conservative
   (c) Catechism
   (d) Fundamentalist

Activities

Complete the answers to these questions:

1 Outline **three** different interpretations of the authority of the Bible.

Some Christians are fundamentalists — they believe that the Bible is not only the Word of God but also the words of God. Some Christians are conservatives and believe that the Bible is the revealed word of God but not his actual words. Some Christians are liberals, they believe

....

....

2 Explain **two** reasons why Catholics regard the Bible as a source of guidance and teaching. In your answer you must refer to a source of wisdom and authority.

Catholics regard the Bible as a source of guidance and teaching because the Church teaches that the Bible is inspired by the Holy Spirit, which means it comes from God and is therefore holy and authoritative because it gives God's truths. As St Paul said in his letter to Timothy, all scripture is inspired by God.

Another reason is

....

....

....

Exam support

You might be asked to evaluate a statement such as: *'You don't need any help to understand the Bible.'* This table might help answer such a question:

Arguments for	Arguments against
• If the Bible is God's word, it must be easy to interpret because God would not confuse us. • You don't need help with the Ten Commandments, they are quite clear — do not steal. • If God sent the Bible to guide and teach us, we must be able to understand it without help.	• Catholics believe the Bible is not always clear in its meaning. • The Church teaches that true Catholic interpretation of the Bible needs help from the Church. • The magisterium of the Church is the teaching office of the Church and gives expert advice on what the Bible means. • The Pope uses papal encyclicals to explain what the Bible means for current situations.

Topic 1.3.3 Scripture, tradition and the magisterium of the Church

REVISED

The Church teaches that the Gospel message of Jesus was handed on in the **Apostolic Tradition** as well as in the writings of the New Testament. The Apostles were given their teachings by Jesus, so the Apostolic Tradition has the true guidance for Christian living.

Catholics believe that Jesus gave St Peter the authority to lead the Church, which was passed to all Popes since then through the **Apostolic Succession**. This means that the tradition from the Apostles has been handed down in the Church through the Pope and the bishops, so the teaching of the Church is unchanged since the Apostles.

The Apostolic Tradition is important because it:
- gives the Church the authority of Jesus
- means the teaching of the Church is the teaching that was given to the Apostles by Jesus
- guarantees that the teaching Catholics follow is correct, true faith.

The Apostolic Succession is important because:
- it means that the Pope today has the same authority that Christ gave to St Peter
- it proves that when the Pope and the bishops give the teaching of the Church in the magisterium, they speak as the successors of the Apostles chosen by Jesus.

The magisterium is when the Pope and the bishops act as interpreters of the Bible and Apostolic Tradition. Their task is to interpret the Bible for twenty-first-century Catholics and define the beliefs of the Catholic Church.
- The ordinary magisterium is when the bishops teach what has always been taught.
- The **conciliar magisterium** is when the Pope calls a general council to decide teachings (for example Vatican II).
- The **pontifical** magisterium is when the Pope uses **papal infallibility** to decide a doctrine (the last time was when Pope Pius XII declared the **assumption of the Virgin Mary**).

The magisterium is important for Catholics because:
- there is no higher authority for Catholics than the magisterium
- it gives Catholics answers to issues that did not exist in the time of the Apostles, for example same-sex partnerships
- it provides clear guidelines for Catholics on what to believe and how to behave as Catholics in today's world.

The role of the Pope in the Catholic Church is to:
- lead the worldwide Church and make sure it is cared for
- organise the magisterium and make sure it is kept up to date
- appoint and ordain new cardinals and bishops, and make sure their teaching is correct
- give guidance to Catholics about current issues.

Apostolic Succession The line of bishops going back to the Apostles.

Apostolic Tradition The oral Gospel passed on by the Apostles to the Church.

Assumption of the Virgin Mary The belief that Mary was assumed body and soul into heaven.

Conciliar magisterium The Church meeting and working as a Council of Bishops with the Pope.

Papal infallibility When the Pope speaks authoritatively on a disputed matter of doctrine.

Pontifical Relating to the office of the Pope as the head of the Church.

Sources of wisdom and authority

The Catechism says, 'The task of interpreting the word of God authentically has been entrusted solely to the Magisterium, that is to the Pope and bishops in communion with him.'

The Catechism teaches that it is the Magisterium's task to preserve God's people from error and so has been given the charism of infallibility in matters of faith and morals.

Now test yourself

1 Apostolic Tradition means:
   (a) Relating to the office of the Pope as the head of the Church
   (b) The oral Gospel passed on by the Apostles to the Church
   (c) The line of bishops going back to the Apostles
   (d) The Church meeting and working as a Council of Bishops with the Pope
2 Apostolic Succession means:
   (a) Relating to the office of the Pope as the head of the Church
   (b) The oral Gospel passed on by the Apostles to the Church
   (c) The line of bishops going back to the Apostles
   (d) The Church meeting and working as a Council of Bishops with the Pope
3 Conciliar magisterium means:
   (a) Relating to the office of the Pope as the head of the Church
   (b) The oral Gospel passed on by the Apostles to the Church
   (c) The line of bishops going back to the Apostles
   (d) The Church meeting and working as a Council of Bishops with the Pope
4 Pontifical means:
   (a) Relating to the office of the Pope as the head of the Church
   (b) The oral Gospel passed on by the Apostles to the Church
   (c) The line of bishops going back to the Apostles
   (d) The Church meeting and working as a Council of Bishops with the Pope

Activities

Complete the answers to these questions:
1 Outline the **three** different levels of magisterium.

The ordinary magisterium is when the bishops teach what has always been taught. The conciliar magisterium is when the Pope calls a general council to decide teachings (for example Vatican II). Pontifical magisterium is when

....

....

2 Explain **two** reasons why the magisterium is important for Catholics. In your answer you must refer to a source of wisdom and authority.

The magisterium is important for Catholics because there is no higher authority for Catholics than the magisterium. As the Catechism says, 'the task of interpreting the word of God authentically has been entrusted solely to the magisterium.'

Another reason is

....

....

....

Exam support

You might be asked to evaluate a statement such as: *'The magisterium is the only authority Christians need.'* This table might help answer such a question:

Arguments for	Arguments against
• The Catechism says it was given the task of interpreting God's word by God. • There is no higher authority for Catholics than the magisterium. • It gives Catholics answers to issues that did not exist in the time of the Apostles, for example same-sex partnerships. • It provides clear guidelines for Catholics on what to believe and how to behave as Catholics in today's world.	• Christianity is based on Jesus so Christians need the Gospels which record Jesus' life. • The magisterium is based on the Scriptures, so Christians need the Bible. • Events happen which are not covered by the magisterium, so Christians need the Pope to issue encyclicals. • The Church needs a leader with authority and so Christians need the Pope as well as the magisterium.

Topic 1.3.4 The Second Vatican Council

When Pope John XXIII become Pope in 1958, the world had changed after the second World War and so he called the Second Vatican Council to:

- bring the Church up to date (*aggiornamento*)
- open the Church to 'the wind of the Holy Spirit'
- bring the leadership of the Church closer to the people.

The Council produced four documents.

The Sacred Council (Sacrosanctum Concilium) proposed changes to worship:

- There was to be a new, simpler rite of the Mass in the language of the local people (**vernacular**).
- The **laity** were to be allowed to do parts of the Bible readings and lead the bidding prayers.
- Priests could face the people during Mass.

The Light of Humanity (Lumen Gentium) proposed changes to the nature of the Church:

- Rather than a pyramid with the Pope at the top descending down to the people at the base, the Church should be a circle, with the people joined together but with the Pope and the bishops leading and holding things together.
- Every Christian (not just priests) is called to serve Christ, in the world, and all the baptised are part of the priesthood (**common priesthood**).
- The ordained priesthood (**sacramental priesthood**) is taken from the common priesthood to celebrate the sacraments.

'Joy and hope' (Gaudium et Spes) was addressed to the whole world and:

- affirmed the human rights and dignity of each person
- expressed concern over morals and values in the changing world
- claimed that peace and justice are necessary for all, whatever their belief
- encouraged dialogue with atheists and secular groups for social action and change.

'The Word of God' (Dei Verbum) said that:

- the Bible should be read by Catholics in their own language
- Catholics should read the Bible and apply its teachings to their lives.

The Council also declared that:

- Protestants and other Christians should be known as **separated brethren**
- Catholics should pray with other Christians to work for greater unity
- Communion should not be shared without a greater unity in the faith
- the fullness of the Church resided in the Roman Catholic Church, in communion with the Pope as the successor of St Peter.

Different understandings of the importance of the Council

- Many Catholics saw the Second Vatican Council as a great relief and encouragement as the Church listened to the people and opened up to the modern world.
- Some thought the reforms of Vatican II went too far and wanted to keep aspects such as the Tridentine Mass (the Latin Eucharistic liturgy used by the Roman Catholic Church from 1570 to 1964).
- Some thought the changes did not go far enough – there should be married priests, changes in Church teachings about contraception, shared communion with non-Catholic Christians and allowing divorced and remarried people to take communion.

Common priesthood All the baptised who follow Christ and serve him.

Laity All the people of the Church who are not chosen to be bishops, priests or deacons.

Sacramental priesthood The ordained priests who lead and celebrate Mass and the sacraments.

Separated brethren Non-Catholic Christians.

Vernacular The language of the people.

Sources of wisdom and authority

The documents produced by Vatican II carry the authority of the Church.

Now test yourself

1 Common priesthood is:
   (a) Italian for bringing something up to date
   (b) All the baptised who follow Christ and serve him
   (c) The language of the people
   (d) The ordained priests who lead and celebrate Mass and the sacraments

2 Sacramental priesthood is:
   (a) Italian for bringing something up to date
   (b) All the baptised who follow Christ and serve him
   (c) The language of the people
   (d) The ordained priests who lead and celebrate Mass and the sacraments

3 Vernacular is:
   (a) Italian for bringing something up to date
   (b) All the baptised who follow Christ and serve him
   (c) The language of the people
   (d) The ordained priests who lead and celebrate Mass and the sacraments

4 *Aggiornamento* is:
   (a) Italian for bringing something up to date
   (b) All the baptised who follow Christ and serve him
   (c) The language of the people
   (d) The ordained priests who lead and celebrate Mass and the sacraments

Activities

Complete the answers to these questions:

1 Outline **three** important documents from the Second Vatican Council.

One important document from Vatican II was *Joy and Hope*, which affirmed the dignity of all people. Another important document was *The Light of Humanity*, which proposed changes to the nature of the Church. A third important document from Vatican II was the sacred council which proposed changes to worship.

2 Explain **two** reasons why the Second Vatican Council was important for Catholics. In your answer you must refer to a source of wisdom and authority.

Vatican II was important for Catholics because it produced the document 'The Sacred Council' (*Sacrosanctum Concilium*), which introduced a new, simpler rite of the Mass in the vernacular, the language of the local people.

A second reason was that the document 'The Nature of the Church' (*Lumen Gentium*) increased the role of the laity so that instead of the Church being like a pyramid, with the Pope at the top descending down to the people at the base, now the Church was to be a circle, with the people joined together but with the pope and bishops leading and holding things together.

Exam support

You might be asked to evaluate a statement such as: *'The most important decision of Vatican II was to allow the Mass to be in English instead of Latin.'* This table might help answer such a question:

Arguments for	Arguments against
● The Mass is the most important sacrament for Catholics but they could not understand what was happening. ● The Mass in English brought the Mass alive for English-speaking Catholics. ● The Mass in English allowed the laity to be part of the Mass rather than just onlookers. ● It allowed young Catholics and non-Catholics to begin to understand the importance of the Mass and maybe want to come into the Church.	It was just as important that: ● Catholics could read the Bible in their own language. ● every Christian was called to serve Christ, not just priests. ● Catholics were encouraged to pray with other Christians and seek greater unity. ● Catholics should enter dialogue with atheists and secular groups for social change.

Topic 1.3.5 The Church as the Body of Christ and the People of God

The Church as the Body of Christ means that:
- all Christians carry on Christ's work on Earth
- Christians are united with each other and with Christ through baptism, making them members of Christ's body
- all Catholics receive the Body of Christ in the Mass, which joins them with all the other Christians around the world receiving the sacrament
- just as the parts of the human body are interdependent, so in the Body of Christ all are interdependent and none is superior, so there should be no division in the body.

Why the Church as the Body of Christ is important for Catholics

- This is how the Church is described in the New Testament and the Catechism.
- It means that Christ did not leave the Earth at his ascension; his body remained on the Earth in the Church.
- It means that the Church is carrying on the work of Christ in the world.
- It means that Christians form one body and so are united with each other as well as with Christ.
- It explains the importance of the Mass. By sharing the consecrated host at Communion, Catholics share in the Body of Christ and renew their membership of Christ's Body.
- It shows how Christians can continue the helping and teaching work of Jesus today because they are the Body of Christ on Earth.
- It shows how Christians can perform different tasks and yet be a unity. There can be different talents and tasks (just as the body has different limbs and organs) and yet the Church remains a unity because all are working together as the Body of Christ.

The Church is also the People of God. Before Christ, God called the Jewish people to be his people and his witnesses to the world. Now in Christ, God has called people from all the nations of the world to join together in the Body of Christ to become the People of God – God's witnesses to the world.

Different Christian understandings of these ideas

Although all Christians believe the Church is the Body of Christ and the People of God, there are different ideas about its structure, leadership and authority:
- Catholic Christians accept the authority of the Pope and believe it is the role of the Pope to rule and guide the Church and to pass on the true teachings of Christ.
- **Orthodox** Christians reject the authority of the Pope and believe authority comes from councils of bishops or **patriarchs** acting together.
- Protestant Christians believe the Bible is the sole authority, the Pope has no authority to decide on beliefs and Churches should be ruled democratically.

The **Ecumenical Movement** believes that the teachings of St Paul mean Christians should unite as the Body of Christ, and Protestants and Orthodox Christians have come together in the World Council of Churches. The Catholic Church in England and Wales is working as a member of Churches Together to show the unity of Christians in action.

Ecumenical Movement Movement working for co-operation between the Churches and eventual Church unity.

Orthodox Churches National Churches which are in the union with the Patriarch of Constantinople.

Patriarch The highest-ranking bishop in Orthodox Christianity.

Sources of wisdom and authority

St Paul said in Romans 12 that although there are many Christians, Christians are one body in Christ and so are members of one another.

The Catechism says that the Church is the Body of Christ, and in the sacraments, especially the Eucharist, Christ establishes the community of believers as his own body.

Now test yourself

1 All the people of the Church who are not chosen to be bishops, priests or deacons are known as:
   (a) The ordained
   (b) Presbyters
   (c) The laity
   (d) The diaconate

2 National Churches which are in the union with the Patriarch of Constantinople are known as:
   (a) Methodist
   (b) Pentecostal
   (c) Baptist
   (d) Orthodox

3 The highest-ranking bishop in Orthodox Christianity is the:
   (a) Pope
   (b) Primate
   (c) Patriarch
   (d) President

4 The Catholic Church refers to non-Catholic Christians as:
   (a) Plymouth Brethren
   (b) Separated Brethren
   (c) Exclusive Brethren
   (d) Our Brethren

Activities

Complete the answers to these questions:

1 Outline **three** meanings of the Church as the Body of Christ.

One meaning of the Church as the Body of Christ is that all Christians carry on Christ's work on Earth. Another meaning is that Christians are united with each other and with Christ through baptism. A third meaning is that

recieving the body of christ in Mass, joins the people with all the christians around the world receiving the sacrament.

2 Explain **two** reasons why Christians call the Church the Body of Christ. In your answer you must refer to a source of wisdom and authority.

One reason is that it is what the New Testament calls the Church. As St Paul said in Romans 12, although there are many Christians, Christians are one body in Christ and so are members of one another.

Another reason is

that it means that christ did not leave the Earth at his acension, his body remained on the Earth in the church.

Exam support

You might be asked to evaluate a statement such as: *'The Christian Church does not deserve to be called Christ's Body.'* This table might help answer such a question:

Arguments for	Arguments against
● The Christian Church is divided (for example Protestants and Catholics) whereas a body is united. ● Most Church members do not behave like Christ, which they should if they were carrying on his work. ● The Church does not appear to be Christ's body because it is rich but he was poor. ● The Church does not seem like Christ's body because it has power and political influence, but Christ rejected power and influence.	● This is how the Church is described in the New Testament and the Catechism. ● The Church is carrying on the work of Christ in the world. ● By sharing the consecrated host at communion, Christians share in the Body of Christ and renew their membership of Christ's body. ● Christians continue the helping and teaching work of Jesus today because they are the Body of Christ on Earth.

Topic 1.3.5 The Church as the Body of Christ and the People of God

Topic 1.3.6 The four marks of the Church

In the Nicene Creed, Christians say, 'I believe in one, holy, catholic and apostolic Church.' These are the four marks of the Church.

Catholics believe the Church is one because:
- the Church is based on one Lord, Jesus Christ
- the Church has one baptism for the forgiveness of sins
- the Church is inspired by one Spirit
- the Church has one faith as agreed in the Creeds.

Catholics believe the Church is holy because:
- God made it, therefore it belongs to God, and so his Church is holy
- Christ gave his life to make his Church holy; his Church is devoted to God
- the Church is the source of the sacraments, which bring God's grace to humanity, therefore it is empowered by God and so is holy
- the Church has been given the true faith and is guided by the Holy Spirit, therefore it holy.

Catholic means universal. Catholics believe the Church is catholic because:
- whereas the Jewish religion was for one race, Christianity is for the whole world – the Christian Church includes people from all over the world
- the Christian message is for everyone, whatever their race, gender or colour
- the Christian message can be understood and believed by anyone, wherever they are in the world.

Catholics believe the Church is apostolic because:
- it was founded by the Apostles
- it received the **Apostolic Tradition** and so teaches what the Apostles taught
- the bishops are the successors of the Apostles who maintain and proclaim the message of Jesus
- the authority of St Peter has been passed down by the **Apostolic Succession** to the current Pope.

The four marks are important because they remind Catholics that:
- there is one faith and the Catholic Church has preserved that faith
- the Church does not belong to any one nation or culture
- the Church traces itself back to the Apostles through the line of bishops
- the Church is holy, it comes from God.

How the four marks may be understood in different ways by Christians today

- Protestants see the oneness of the Church as based on the Bible and **Creeds**. For Catholics and Orthodox it is based on the Creeds and **Catechism**.
- All Christians agree that the Church is holy.
- All Christians agree that the Church is catholic as it is for all races and nations.
- Protestants believe the Church is apostolic because it is based on the Bible. For Catholics and Orthodox it is also based on Apostolic Tradition and the line of bishops.

Apostolic Succession The line of bishops going back to the Apostles.

Apostolic Tradition The faith taught by Jesus and the Apostles.

Catechism The official teaching of the Church.

Catholic Universal.

Creed Statement of Christian beliefs.

Sources of wisdom and authority

Jesus said in Matthew's Gospel, 'You are Peter and on this rock I will build my Church and the gates of hell will not overcome it. I will give you the keys of the kingdom of heaven; whatever you bind on earth will be bound in heaven, and whatever you loose on earth will be loosed in heaven.'

'I believe in One, Holy, Catholic and Apostolic Church.' Nicene Creed.

Now test yourself and Activities answers at www.hoddereducation.co.uk/myrevisionnotes

Now test yourself

1 The line of bishops going back to the Apostles is known as the:
(a) Creed
(b) Catechism
(c) Apostolic Tradition
(d) Apostolic Succession

2 The faith taught by Jesus and the Apostles is known as the:
(a) Creed
(b) Catechism
(c) Apostolic Tradition
(d) Apostolic Succession

3 The official teaching of the Church is known as the:
(a) Creed
(b) Catechism
(c) Apostolic Tradition
(d) Apostolic Succession

4 A statement of Christian beliefs is known as the:
(a) Creed
(b) Catechism
(c) Apostolic Tradition
(d) Apostolic Succession

Activities

Complete the answers to these questions:

1 Outline the **four** marks of the Church.

The four marks of the Church are stated in the belief in the Nicene Creed which says that the Church is One, the Church is

holy, the Church means catholic and the church is apostolic
God made it, belongs to God   Jewith religion I race   founded by the apostles
Christianity for all

2 Explain why the Apostolic Succession is important for Catholics. In your answer you must refer to a source of wisdom and authority.

The Apostolic Succession is important for Catholics because it means that the Pope today has the same authority that Christ gave to St Peter when he said in Matthew's Gospel, 'You are Peter and on this rock I will build my Church and the gates of hell will not overcome it. I will give you the keys of the kingdom of heaven; whatever you bind on earth will be bound in heaven, and whatever you loose on earth will be loosed in heaven.'

Another reason is

Thit recieved the apostolic tradition and so teaches that what the Apostles taughts, the bishops are the successors of the Apostles who maintain and proclaim the message of Jesus.

Exam support

You might be asked to evaluate a statement such as: *'The Church is too divided for it to be called One and Holy.'* This table might help answer such a question:

Arguments for	Arguments against
● The Church is not one because it is divided into Catholic, Orthodox and Protestant. ● The Church is not one because it has different attitudes to the Bible — fundamentalists, liberals, etc. ● The Church is not one because it has different attitudes to issues such as abortion and contraception. ● The Church is not holy because some Churches say gay people are evil and refuse the sacraments to them and to people who are divorced.	● The Church is one because it has one baptism for the forgiveness of sins. ● The Church is one because it has one faith as agreed in the Creeds. ● The Church is holy because it is the source of the sacraments, therefore it is empowered by God. ● The Church is holy because it has been given the true faith and is guided by the Holy Spirit.

Topic 1.3.7 Mary as a model of the Church

The Virgin Mary is a model of the Church because:
- as the mother of Christ, she gave him to the world: Catholics believe the Church should show Christ to the world
- she was the mother of Christ and the Church is like a mother to believers as they find new life through baptism from the Church
- by her **assumption** into heaven, she shows that the Church will bring faithful Christians into heaven.

Mary is a model of Christian discipleship because:
- she obeyed God's plan for her: she did not question what was to happen to her
- she was conceived without sin (**immaculate conception**) and continued to be sinless throughout her life. By following her example, Catholics can also try to live pure lives
- she showed complete devotion to Jesus – she loved her son and was with him right to the end, even sharing in his sufferings on the cross
- she was always a help and support to her son – for example, at the wedding feast in Cana she told the people to ask Jesus and to 'do whatever he tells you'.

Mary is an example of faith because:
- she believed the message of the Angel Gabriel at the **Annunciation** even though she had no proof that it would happen
- she believed that Jesus was God's Son before he performed any miracles simply because of what Gabriel had said
- she trusted that God would make sure death was not the end for her son.

Mary is an example of charity because:
- she gave up her own life/career to bear God's son when she could have refused
- she was always ready to help people
- she continues to pray for those who need her help.

The teachings about Mary are important for Catholic life today because:
- she had an immaculate conception – this means that Jesus was totally sinless because his mother was born without original sin and his father was God
- if she had not obeyed God, Jesus would not have been born and without his birth there would be no Christianity and no salvation
- the virgin birth means Mary gave birth to God and so she is 'the mother of God' – as such, she must be the most important human being ever to have lived
- at the end of her life, she was taken up to heaven instead of dying (the assumption of the Blessed Virgin Mary), so she did not suffer death like everyone else
- in heaven, she is able to pray for the souls of Christians on Earth, so she can make the prayers of Catholics more effective and give them more chance of God's help.

Annunciation The greeting of Gabriel when he told Mary she was to have a son who would be the Christ.

Assumption The belief that the Virgin Mary was taken into heaven body and soul.

Immaculate conception The belief that the Virgin Mary was conceived without original sin and was always full of grace.

Theotokos The Greek description of Mary as the 'God bearer'.

Sources of wisdom and authority

'I am the Lord's servant,' Mary answered. 'May your word to me be fulfilled.' Mary's answer at the Annunciation.

'Mary, Mother of Christ, Mother of the Church.' Catechism of the Catholic Church.

'By her complete adherence to the Father's will, to his Son's redemptive work, and to every prompting of the Holy Spirit, the Virgin Mary is the Church's model of faith and charity.' Catechism of the Catholic Church.

Now test yourself

1 The Annunciation is:
(a) The Greek description of Mary as the 'God bearer'
(b) The belief that the Virgin Mary was taken into heaven body and soul
(c) The greeting of Gabriel when he told Mary she was to have a son who would be the Christ
(d) The belief that the Virgin Mary was conceived without original sin and was always full of grace

2 The assumption is:
(a) The Greek description of Mary as the 'God bearer'
(b) The belief that the Virgin Mary was taken into heaven body and soul
(c) The greeting of Gabriel when he told Mary she was to have a son who would be the Christ
(d) The belief that the Virgin Mary was conceived without original sin and was always full of grace

3 The immaculate conception is:
(a) The Greek description of Mary as the 'God bearer'
(b) The belief that the Virgin Mary was taken into heaven body and soul
(c) The greeting of Gabriel when he told Mary she was to have a son who would be the Christ
(d) The belief that the Virgin Mary was conceived without original sin and was always full of grace

Activities

Complete the answers to these questions:

1 Outline **three** Catholic beliefs about the Virgin Mary.

Catholics believe that the Virgin Mary is a model of faith and charity. They also believe she had an immaculate conception. Another belief is *that Mary is a model of Christian discipleship as she obeyed God's plan for her.*

2 Explain **two** reasons why Catholics believe Mary is a model of discipleship. In your answer you must refer to a source of wisdom and authority.

Catholics believe Mary is a model of Christian discipleship because she obeyed God's plan for her: she did not question what was to happen to her. At the Annunciation, Luke's Gospel says Mary replied to the Angel Gabriel, 'I am the Lord's servant, may your word to me be fulfilled.'

Another reason is *is that she showed complete devotion to Jesus – she loved her son and was with him right to the end, even sharing in his sufferings on the cross.*

Exam support

You might be asked to evaluate a statement such as: 'The Virgin Mary has too much importance for Catholics.' This table might help answer such a question:

Arguments for	Arguments against
● Catholics offer prayers through the Virgin Mary, but the Bible says prayers should only be offered through Jesus. ● The belief in the immaculate conception and the assumption make Mary appear semi-divine, but there is no reference to them in the Bible. ● Catholics regard Mary as the model of Christian discipleship, but there is very little about Mary's life. In the Gospels Jesus is the model of Christian discipleship.	● If Mary had not obeyed God, Jesus would not have been born and without his birth there would be no Christianity and no salvation. ● The virgin birth means Mary gave birth to God and so she is 'the mother of God'. As the mother of God, Mary must be the most important human being ever to have lived. ● At the end of her life she did not suffer human death, but was taken up to heaven she is able to pray for the souls of Christians on Earth.

Topic 1.3.8 Sources of personal and ethical decision-making

Catholics use a few sources of guidance when making moral decisions.

The example and teaching of Jesus

Catholics would look at the life of Jesus (God made man) to see what he would have done, Jesus' teaching, which is summed by the **Golden Rule** 'Do to others as you would have them do to you', and the greatest commandments 'Love God and love your neighbour as yourself'.

Christians believe Jesus fulfilled the Law of Moses in the New Law of Christ, summed up in the **Sermon on the Mount** which is based on love of God and love of neighbour.

The natural law

Natural law is the moral order designed by God at the creation so that if people work in harmony with natural law, they will be living as they should. The Catholic Church teaches that the order of creation is the natural order (natural law), which can be seen by human reason and which must be followed by Christians because it is what God established. For example, marriage between a man and a woman is the natural order because it creates a family and ensures the continuation of the human race (so same-sex marriage is wrong because it is against natural law).

However, people can be mistaken about the voice of God and could be mistaken about the voice of conscience.

Conscience

The Church teaches that the voice of **conscience** is the voice of God, therefore Christians should follow it. St Paul and St Thomas Aquinas taught that Christians should use their conscience as the final part of moral decision-making. Christians should follow their conscience if it tells them the Church is wrong (for example on artificial contraception), since conscience is God speaking directly to individuals. However, many Christians are doubtful about relying on conscience because people can be mistaken about the voice of God and could be mistaken about the voice of conscience.

The teachings of the Church

Most Catholics would use the teachings of the magisterium as authoritative guidance because it is the guidance given by the Pope and bishops inspired by the Holy Spirit.

Implications for Christians today

Christians often use more than one authority when making a moral decision because:
- the example and teaching of Jesus say nothing about modern issues such as contraception or same-sex marriage
- Some Catholics might use their conscience to make decisions about same-sex marriage or supplying condoms to AIDS sufferers.
- Others might use the authority of Jesus or the Church to reject their conscience.

Conscience An inner feeling of the rightness or wrongness of an action.

Golden Rule The teaching of Jesus that you should treat others as you would like them to treat you.

Natural law The inbuilt moral order to the universe.

Sermon on the Mount Jesus' description of Christian living.

Sources of wisdom and authority

Jesus said in the Sermon on the Mount, 'Do not come to think that I have come to abolish the law or the prophets; I have come not to abolish but to fulfil.'

The Catechism says that natural law expresses the moral sense God has given people to see by reason the difference between good and evil, truth and lie.

The Catechism says it is important for Christians to hear and follow the voice of his conscience.

Now test yourself

1 The Golden Rule is:
   (a) An inner feeling of the rightness or wrongness of an action
   (b) The teaching of Jesus that you should treat others as you would like them to treat you
   (c) The inbuilt moral order to the universe
   (d) Jesus' description of Christian living
2 Natural law is:
   (a) An inner feeling of the rightness or wrongness of an action
   (b) The teaching of Jesus that you should treat others as you would like them to treat you
   (c) The inbuilt moral order to the universe
   (d) Jesus' description of Christian living
3 Conscience is:
   (a) An inner feeling of the rightness or wrongness of an action
   (b) The teaching of Jesus that you should treat others as you would like them to treat you
   (c) The inbuilt moral order to the universe
   (d) Jesus' description of Christian living
4 The Sermon on the Mount is:
   (a) An inner feeling of the rightness or wrongness of an action
   (b) The teaching of Jesus that you should treat others as you would like them to treat you
   (c) The inbuilt moral order to the universe
   (d) Jesus' description of Christian living

Activities

Complete the answers to these questions:

1 Outline **three** sources of personal and ethical decision-making for Catholics.

One source is the teaching and example of Jesus, as found in the four Gospels. A second source is the natural law, which is deduced by reason from the created world. A third source is
conscience the inner feeling that should be followed, the voice of God.

2 Explain **two** reasons why natural law is important for Catholics. In your answer you must refer to a source of wisdom and authority.

Natural law is important for Catholics because it is the moral order designed by God at the creation. Also the Church teaches this is the natural order which must be followed by Christians.

Another reason is that the Catechism says
that the natural law expresses the moral sense God has given people to see by reason the difference between good and evil, truth and lie.

Exam support

You might be asked to evaluate a statement such as: *'You only need the two great commandments of Jesus to make moral decisions.'* This table might help answer such a question:

Arguments for	Arguments against
• If something fits with loving God and loving your neighbour, it must be right. • Christians should do only what will produce good results, and loving God and loving your neighbour will produce good results. • In any situation you can work out what to do by determining what will produce the greatest love for your neighbour. • If you love God, you will always do what God wants and that must be good.	• The Church knows better what Christians should do than an individual Christian and we should make moral decisions on the basis of the magisterium. • It is better to use the Ten Commandments and the Sermon on the Mount rather than relying on our own ideas about what will be loving our neighbour. • Moral decisions need to be based on what all Catholics would agree to, not how an individual Catholic interprets the two commandments.

1.4 Forms of expression and ways of life

Topic 1.4.1 The architecture, design and decoration of Catholic churches

REVISED

Exteriors of Catholic churches can vary in style greatly, but internally most will have:

- a **nave** where the worshippers sit
- a **sanctuary** with the altar (with candles), **lectern** and usually the **tabernacle** (though this could be in a side chapel)
- the baptismal font containing holy water
- a confessional for the sacrament of reconciliation
- a statue of the Sacred Heart of Jesus
- a statue of St Peter holding the keys of the kingdom
- statues of the saints.

Different forms of architecture, design and decoration

- In much older churches the sanctuary is separated from the people and often elevated, reflecting pre-Vatican II ideas.
- Architectural styles differ; for example Westminster Cathedral (the largest Catholic cathedral in England) is Neo-Byzantine, reflecting the late Victorian/Edwardian era when it was built, whereas Liverpool Metropolitan Cathedral is built with concrete and aluminium, reflecting the era when it was constructed, the 1960s.

How the features reflect belief

The altar reflects the belief that the priest offers Mass on the altar as a symbol of Christ offering himself as a sacrifice to God on the cross.

The candles reflect the belief that Jesus is the light of the world.

The tabernacle reflects the belief that Jesus is really present in the Blessed Sacrament.

The baptismal font at the entrance of the church reflects the belief that baptism is what makes a person a member of the Church.

The lectern reflects the belief that faith and truth come from the Bible (the readings) and the teaching of the Church (the homily).

The Sacred Heart symbolises the eternal fire of God's love in Christ.

How the features are used in worship

The focus of Catholic worship is the Mass:

- The people gather in the nave for worship.
- The priests and servers gather in the sanctuary.
- The lectern is used for the Liturgy of the Word.
- The altar is used for the Mass when the gifts are placed on it and then consecrated as the priest offers the sacrifice of Christ.
- The **Blessed Sacrament** is placed in the tabernacle and worshippers genuflect to them on entering the church.

Blessed Sacrament Consecrated hosts kept in the tabernacle.

Lectern Raised stand from which the Bible is read.

Nave The main worship and seating area.

Sanctuary The sacred space where the altar is and where Mass is celebrated.

Tabernacle Where the Blessed Sacrament is kept in Catholic churches.

Sources of wisdom and authority

The Catechism says that the People of God should build a church for worship wherever the authorities allow it.

The Catechism says that a church is a house of prayer in which the Eucharist is celebrated and reserved, where the faithful assemble, and where Jesus Christ is worshipped.

Now test yourself

1 The main worship and seating area is the:
   (a) Lectern
   (b) Nave
   (c) Sanctuary
   (d) Tabernacle

2 The rasied stand from which the Bible is read is the:
   (a) Lectern
   (b) Nave
   (c) Sanctuary
   (d) Tabernacle

3 The sacred space where the altar is and where mass is celebrated is the:
   (a) Lectern
   (b) Nave
   (c) Sanctuary
   (d) Tabernacle

4 The Blessed Sacrament in Catholic churches is kept in the:
   (a) Lectern
   (b) Nave
   (c) Sanctuary
   (d) Tabernacle

Activities

Complete the answers to these questions:

1 Outline **three** design features of a Catholic church.

A Catholic church will be designed to have a nave where the worshippers sit. It will also have a confessional where the sacrament of reconciliation takes place. A third feature will be a sanctuary containing

....

2 Explain **two** ways in which the architecture of a Catholic church reflects Catholic beliefs. In your answer you must refer to a source of wisdom and authority.

The sanctuary with the altar and tabernacle reflects Catholic belief in the importance of the Mass and in transubstantiation. The Catechism says a church is where the Eucharist is celebrated and reserved.

Also the baptismal font at the entrance of the church reflects the belief that

....

....

Exam support

You might be asked to evaluate a statement such as: *'The design of Catholic churches helps people to worship God properly.'* This table might help answer such a question:

Arguments for	Arguments against
● The nave provides a good place for the congregation to take part in the Mass.	● Putting the worshippers together in the nave can be distracting as people watch the people in the congregation rather than worshipping God.
● The sanctuary provides the altar which is central for the Liturgy of the Eucharist as the priest consecrates the hosts and offers the sacrifice of Christ.	● The sanctuary being cut off from the congregation can make it difficult for the congregation to join in the worship of the liturgy.
● The lectern is essential for the Liturgy of the Word when God's word is read and interpreted in the priest's homily.	● You could use any sort of flat surface to celebrate Mass and Catholic beliefs about transubstantiation would not be affected.
● The Blessed Sacrament is placed in the tabernacle as a focus of worship for individuals coming into church.	● The readings and the homily could be given by a priest sitting among the congregation and it would not affect the beliefs or worship.

Topic 1.4.2 The different internal features of a Catholic church

The Catechism says that a Catholic church should contain a baptistry, a holy water font, a confessional and a chair (cathedra) for the bishop and priest. However, there are several features you need to concentrate on.

The lectern for the Bible readings should be suitable for the dignity of God's Word. It is the Gospel reading which clearly expresses the nature and importance of the redemption Christ brought. The Gospel can be read only by an ordained deacon or a priest, or a bishop who represents Christ and so can proclaim his words and deeds. The Bible readings facilitate (help) Catholic worship because they are the basis of the Liturgy of the Word in the Mass.

The **altar** is made of stone that has been consecrated by a bishop and should be at the centre of the church. It expresses the importance of redemption because it is an altar of sacrifice. In the Mass, the sacrifice of Christ on the cross is brought into the present, right among the people, so that Christ's redemption still affects people today. As the Catechism says, 'the sacrifice of Christ offered once for all on the cross remains ever present'. It also helps Catholic worship because it is central to the Eucharist as it is at the altar that **transubstantiation** occurs.

All Catholic churches have a **crucifix** (a cross with an image of Christ on it). The crucifix reminds worshippers of Christ's redemption – Jesus died to save them from sin. It also helps with worship, either alone thanking God for Christ's redemption, or in the Mass helping people to focus on Christ's sacrifice.

The **tabernacle** is a container for **consecrated hosts** (wafers transformed in the Mass) which remind Catholics of the redemption brought by Christ's sacrifice in his body broken for them. The tabernacle also helps with worship because Catholics believe there is a holy and special presence in a church building that keeps the hosts in the tabernacle.

A Catholic church is more than a building or a meeting hall; it is a place of worship where Catholics celebrate the redemption brought to the world by Jesus Christ.

Altar The place where the bread and wine are consecrated. It is a place of sacrifice and a table of sharing.

Consecrated hosts Wafers which have been transformed in the Mass.

Crucifix A cross with an image of Christ on it.

Lectern Raised platform where the Bible is read aloud.

Tabernacle A container for consecrated hosts.

Transubstantiation The belief that the bread and wine change into the body and blood of Christ in an unseen way.

Sources of wisdom and authority

The Catechism says the altar is the centre of the church where the sacrifice of the cross is made present and from which the sacraments flow.

The Catechism says the visible church (building) is a symbol of the Father's house towards which Christians are journeying.

The Catechism says the tabernacle should be in a most worthy place and treated with the greatest honour.

Now test yourself

1 The place where the bread and wine are consecrated is the:
   (a) Consecrated hosts
   (b) Altar
   (c) Crucifix
   (d) Tabernacle
2 The wafers transformed in the Mass are called the:
   (a) Consecrated hosts
   (b) Altar
   (c) Crucifix
   (d) Tabernacle

3 A cross with an image of Christ on it is called a:
   (a) Consecrated hosts
   (b) Altar
   (c) Crucifix
   (d) Tabernacle
4 A container for consecrated hosts is called:
   (a) Consecrated hosts
   (b) Altar
   (c) Crucifix
   (d) Tabernacle

Activities

Complete the answers to these questions:

1 Outline **three** internal features of a Catholic church.

One feature is the lectern, where the Bible readings take place. Another feature is ....

....

A third feature is ....

....

2 Choose **two** internal features of a Catholic church and explain how they express the importance of redemption. In your answer you must refer to a source of wisdom and authority.

One feature is the altar, which expresses the importance of redemption because it is an altar of sacrifice. In the Mass, the sacrifice of Christ on the cross is brought into the present, right among the people, so that Christ's redemption still affects people today. As the Catechism says, 'the sacrifice of Christ offered once for all on the cross remains ever present'.

Another feature is

....

....

....

Exam support

You might be asked to evaluate a statement such as: *'The tabernacle is the most important feature of a Catholic church.'* This table might help answer such a question:

Arguments for	Arguments against
• The tabernacle contains the consecrated hosts which are the Body of Christ. • The tabernacle is the focus to which worshippers genuflect when they enter the church or pass by the tabernacle. • The tabernacle reminds Catholics of the redemption brought by Christ's sacrifice in his 'body broken for you'. • Catholics believe there is a holy and special presence in a church building that keeps the hosts in the tabernacle.	• The baptistry is more important because without baptism people cannot take the other sacraments. • The altar is more important because this is where transubstantiation occurs. • The altar is more important because this is the focus of the Mass, the most important part of Catholic worship. • The altar is an altar of sacrifice where the sacrifice of Christ on the cross is brought into the present in the Mass so that Christ's redemption still affects people today.

Topic 1.4.3 The meaning and significance of sacred objects within Catholicism

Sacred objects are holy things used in prayer and worship which are always treated with respect. The main sacred objects for Catholics are as follows.

Sacred vessels are the vessels used for the bread and the wine. These are the most holy objects as Catholics believe they hold the body and blood of Christ in sacramental form. These vessels are the **paten** (the plate that holds the priest's host), the **ciborium** (the plate that holds the people's hosts) and the **chalice** (the cup to hold the wine and the water). These are handled with care and washed and wiped clean after each Mass. They are particularly important because they are used for the sacrament of the Eucharist and are crucial to belief in the sacred mystery of transubstantiation.

Some would regard the holy water **stoup** at the entrance to the church as a sacred vessel because it contains water blessed in the name of the Trinity to be used on entering the church as a reminder of baptism and the washing clean from sin through the cross of Christ. It is also a reminder of the promise of eternal life promised in baptism.

Cloths and vestments are sacred objects used as special covers for the altar and lectern and for the priest to wear. There are certain colours for certain seasons of the Church's year. The colour scheme expresses Christian beliefs:

- white or gold for special celebrations such as Christmas and Easter
- green for 'ordinary time' when there are no special celebrations
- red for events involving martyrs (recalling their shed blood), for Good Friday and for the Day of Pentecost to symbolise the fire of the Holy Spirit
- purple for penitence or sorrow, during Advent or Lent.

Sarcophagi are containers for dead bodies. They are often made of stone and displayed in churches because they contain the bones of saints. They reflect Catholic beliefs about saints and the holiness which can be gained through prayer and contemplation next to a saint's **sarcophagus**.

Traditionally hunger cloths were widely used during Lent to depict scenes from the life of Christ and were hung over the **rood screen** in front of the altar. Modern hunger cloths are produced by charities such as CAFOD and relate the life of Christ to themes of justice and peace for reflecting Catholic beliefs about the need for Christians to follow the example of Jesus and fight for world justice and peace.

Sacred objects are not used just in church:

- The chalice, paten and ciborium are used to consecrate and distribute Holy Communion.
- Holy images, statues and crucifixes are used in private devotions and prayer, either in church or at home.
- Holy water is used to bless oneself and can be sprinkled at home too.
- Votive candles are lit to symbolise prayers being offered – a candle is lit and placed on a stand in church or at home.
- Priests wear special vestments outside church for such things as funerals.

Chalice Silver or gold cup for the wine to be consecrated at the Mass.

Ciborium The silver or gold container for the hosts.

Paten A silver or gold plate that has the priest's host.

Rood screen A decorated screen or iron work in front of the sanctuary.

Sarcophagus A stone container for bones.

Stoup A container on the wall to hold holy water.

Vestments Special clothes worn by priests when conducting worship.

Sources of wisdom and authority

The Catechism teaches that, 'All the signs in the liturgical celebrations are related to Christ.'

Now test yourself

1 The silver or gold cup for the wine to be consecrated at the Mass is the:
   (a) Chalice
   (b) Ciborium
   (c) Paten
   (d) Vestments

2 The silver or gold container for the people's hosts is the:
   (a) Chalice
   (b) Ciborium
   (c) Paten
   (d) Vestments

3 A silver or gold plate for the priest's host is the:
   (a) Chalice
   (b) Ciborium
   (c) Paten
   (d) Vestments

4 Special clothes worn by priests when conducting worship are called:
   (a) Chalice
   (b) Ciborium
   (c) Paten
   (d) Vestments

Activities

Complete the answers to these questions:

1 Outline **three** sacred vessels found in a Catholic church.

One sacred vessel is the stoup, which is a container on the wall to hold holy water. Another sacred vessel is a

....

And another sacred vessel is a

....

2 Explain two ways sacred objects express Catholic beliefs. In your answer you must refer to a source of authority.

The holy water stoup at the entrance to the church is a sacred vessel because it contains water blessed in the name of the Trinity to be used on entering the church. It expresses Catholic beliefs about baptism such as the washing clean from sin through the cross of Christ. It is also a reminder of the promise of eternal life promised in baptism. As the Catechism says, 'All the signs in the liturgical celebrations are related to Christ.'

Another sacred object is

....

....

....

Exam support

You might be asked to evaluate a statement such as: *'Sacred objects help Catholics to understand their faith.'* This table might help answer such a question:

Arguments for	Arguments against
• Cloths and vestments help with understanding key events, for example red for Good Friday symbolises Christ's sacrifice, and for the Day of Pentecost to symbolise the fire of the Holy Spirit.	Sacred objects help Catholics express the faith, not understand it. Understanding comes from:
• The sacred vessels of paten, chalice and ciborium help Catholics understand the Eucharist and the transubstantiation that occurs.	• the Gospel readings about Jesus' life and teachings
• The crucifix reminds worshippers of Christ's redemption — Jesus died to save them from sin.	• the priest's homily explaining the faith
• Hunger cloths relate the life of Christ to themes of justice and peace and encourage Catholics to fight for world justice and peace.	• papal encyclicals in which the Pope explains the faith for the contemporary world
	• bishops' letters relating the faith to the society in which Catholics live.

Topic 1.4.3 The meaning and significance of sacred objects within Catholicism

Topic 1.4.4 The meaning and significance of paintings, frescoes and drawing within Catholicism

REVISED

Catholicism has always used images to help people to understand, celebrate and remember Catholic beliefs.

Sacred art uses the form of secular art to:
- express the faith and emotions of the artist
- help the observer understand more about God
- draw the observer into deeper worship of God
- back up the beliefs of the Catholic faith
- give greater insight into the truths of the Catholic faith.

Icon of Christ – St Catherine's Monastery, Sinai

Icons are religious paintings especially connected with Eastern Christianity. This is the oldest known icon of Christ and illustrates many beliefs:
- The different facial expressions on either side of the face show Christ's two natures.
- The halo shows Christ's holiness and the fact it is gold shows his divinity.
- The position of the fingers on the right hand symbolises both the Trinity and Christ's death on the cross.
- The holy book symbolises that Christ is the Word of God and that the Bible comes from God.

Fresco by Giotto of St Francis of Assisi

A fresco is a method of painting on freshly laid plaster so that the colours fuse with the wall. Giotto painted a number of scenes from the life of St Francis of Assisi in the Basilica of St Francis in Assisi, Italy. St Francis was wealthy but gave away all his possessions to become a Franciscan friar.

The fresco shows various beliefs:
- St Francis preaching to the birds shows nature as part of God's creation and birdsong as praising the Creator.
- St Francis' golden halo shows the holy quality of his life and God's presence within him.
- St Francis' one hand lowered symbolises him welcoming the birds.
- The other hand is raised in blessing, with three fingers reflecting the Trinity.

Different ways Catholic art is used to express belief

The Council of Nicaea said that holy images of our Lord and Saviour, Jesus Christ, Mary, the angels and all the saints should be exhibited in churches, on sacred vessels and vestments, on walls and panels, in houses and on streets. The Catholic Church has followed this advice and so sacred art is displayed in a variety of places and ways.

Sacred art is not just for decoration but also acts as an aid to worship. It is not the images themselves that are worshipped but what they represent. Individual believers will not only use the images in church to help their worship, they will also have prayer cards with holy images and pictures on their walls at home.

> **Fresco** A painting rendered on fresh plaster.
>
> **Friar** A wandering preacher who has taken vows of poverty.
>
> **Halo** The golden circle around Christ or a saint's head to show they are holy.
>
> **Icon** A holy image painted in a certain style on wood.
>
> **Secular** Not connected with religious or spiritual matters.

Sources of wisdom and authority

The Catechism teaches that sacred art can evoke faith and adoration by portraying the transcendent mystery of God.

The Catechism teaches that bishops, personally or through delegates, should see to the promotion of sacred art, old and new, in all its forms.

Now test yourself and Activities answers at **www.hoddereducation.co.uk/myrevisionnotes**

1 Secular means:
   (a) A painting rendered on fresh plaster
   (b) A golden circle around Christ or a saint's head to show they are holy
   (c) A holy image painted in a certain style on wood
   (d) Not connected with religious or spiritual matters

2 A fresco is:
   (a) A painting rendered on fresh plaster
   (b) A golden circle around Christ or a saint's head to show they are holy
   (c) A holy image painted in a certain style on wood
   (d) Not connected with religious or spiritual matters

3 An icon is:
   (a) A painting rendered on fresh plaster
   (b) A golden circle around Christ or a saint's head to show they are holy
   (c) A holy image painted in a certain style on wood
   (d) Not connected with religious or spiritual matters

4 A halo is:
   (a) A painting rendered on fresh plaster
   (b) A golden circle around Christ or a saint's head to show they are holy
   (c) A holy image painted in a certain style on wood
   (d) Not connected with religious or spiritual matters

Activities

Complete the answers to these questions:

1 Outline **three** purposes of sacred art for Catholics.

One purpose is to give greater insight into the truths of the Catholic faith. A second purpose is to help the observer understand more about God. A third purpose is to

....

....

2 Explain **three** ways a piece of sacred art portrays Catholic beliefs.

The icon of Christ at St Catherine's Monastery, Sinai portrays Catholic beliefs in the different facial expressions on either side of the face which show Catholic belief in Christ's two natures (human and divine).

The position of the fingers on the right hand portrays Catholic belief in the Trinity and Christ's death on the cross.

The holy book portrays

....

....

Exam support

You might be asked to evaluate a statement such as: *'Paintings help Catholics to understand their relationship with God.'* This table might help answer such a question:

Arguments for	Arguments against
• Artists paint sacred pictures to express their relationship with God and help the observer relate this to their own experience. • Giotto's fresco of St Francis preaching to the birds shows nature as part of God's creation and our relationship with it. • The icon of Christ at St Catherine's Monastery, Sinai shows that God has come close to humanity in Christ who was both human and divine. • Contemplating pictures of the sacred heart helps in understanding God's love for humans and the sacrifice he made for humans.	• Paintings might help us understand beliefs, but our relationship with God is personal and spiritual. • Relationship with God is developed through participating in the sacraments. • Relationship with God is understood through prayer and adoration. • Understanding of our relationship with God is deepened through homilies and advice from priests, bishops and the Pope.

Topic 1.4.4 The meaning and significance of paintings, frescoes and drawing within Catholicism

Topic 1.4.5 The meaning and significance of sculptures and statues

Sculptures and statues are three-dimensional art. The great artists such as Michelangelo used both painting and sculpture. The Catholic Church tends to use more statues in churches as aids to worship whereas the Orthodox Church tends to use paintings in the form of icons. Statues can give a greater feeling of reality and so are easier to use as aids to worship.

Statues are also a good way of expressing beliefs because nothing is hidden or requires interpretation:

- Statues of the Virgin Mary with her baby son (**Madonna** and child) show her pointing to Christ, reflecting the belief that although Mary is the mother of God, she is a witness to her son, who is more important than her.
- Statues of Mary with her adult son portray Mary as young, too young to be the mother of the child she holds, showing that she is her son's daughter as much as he is her son. Christ was her Creator and Redeemer.
- Statues of the Sacred Heart of Jesus are based on visions by St Margaret Mary Alacoque and show the heart of Jesus exposed, surrounded by the crown of thorns with a fire burning within it. The thorns remind Catholics of the Passion of Christ and the fire of his eternal love.
- Bronze statues of St Peter are copies of the one in St Peter's Basilica in Rome. They show St Peter holding up his hand in blessing while the other hand clutches the **keys to the kingdom** of heaven, reflecting the belief that St Peter was the rock on which Christ built his Church and was given the authority to forgive sins (the keys of the kingdom) and that the Popes are the successors of St Peter charged with looking after the Church on Earth.

> **Intercede** To act or pray on behalf of someone in difficulty or trouble.
>
> **Keys to the kingdom** The authority Catholics believe that St Peter (and then the Popes) received from Christ.
>
> **Madonna** A painting or statue of the Virgin Mary.
>
> **Patronal** Relating to a patron saint.
>
> **Votive candle** A candle that is lit as a prayer is offered.

How sculptures and statues may be used

Any Catholic church will usually have a statue of the Sacred Heart of Jesus, the Blessed Virgin Mary, St Peter, the **patronal** saint, and other saints. These statues will not be worshipped but rather will be a focus of prayer. There will be opportunity for **votive candles** to be lit as a further aid to prayer. Many Catholics offer their prayers through the saints. They ask the Virgin Mary or the saints to **intercede** for them so that their prayers have more weight and are more likely to be answered. Many worshippers will touch the foot of St Peter and kiss it in devotion and respect when they enter or leave a church.

Catholic statues are not confined to the inside of a church:

- Most Catholic churches will have a crucifix and probably a Madonna and child in the grounds.
- There may be wayside crosses, crucifixes or Madonnas at crossroads (especially in Catholic countries) as reminders of the faith.
- Any place associated with a saint, vision or special happening will have a statue of the saint and probably a crucifix and/or Madonna to indicate the holiness of the place.

Sources of wisdom and authority

The Catechism explains that human art expresses humans' relationship with God and the way human creativity has a connection with the creativity of God.

St Matthew's Gospel chapter 16 records Jesus choosing St Peter to be the foundation of the Church and giving him the keys of the kingdom.

Now test yourself

1 Intercede means:
   (a) To pray for
   (b) To act or pray on behalf of someone in difficulty or trouble
   (c) Relating to a patron saint
   (d) Relating to Jesus

2 Patronal means:
   (a) To pray for
   (b) To act or pray on behalf of someone in difficulty or trouble
   (c) Relating to a patron saint
   (d) Relating to Jesus

3 Keys of the kingdom refer to:
   (a) The Apostolic Succession
   (b) The authority of Jesus
   (c) The authority Catholics believe that St Peter received from Christ
   (d) The importance of the Catechism

4 Madonna is a name given to:
   (a) A statue of a saint
   (b) A statue of Jesus
   (c) A painting or statue of the Virgin Mary
   (d) A statue of St Peter

Activities

Complete the answers to these questions:

1 Outline **three** statues you are likely to find in a Catholic church.

Most Catholic churches will have a statue of the Virgin Mary. They will also have a statue of the Sacred Heart of Jesus. Another statue you are likely to find is

....

2 Explain **two** ways in which statues express Catholic beliefs. In your answer you must refer to a source of wisdom and authority.

Statues of St Peter show him holding up his hand in blessing while the other hand clutches the keys of the kingdom of heaven, expressing the belief that St Peter was the rock on which Christ built his Church and was given the authority to forgive sins (the keys of the kingdom). St Matthew's Gospel records Jesus choosing St Peter to be the foundation of the Church and giving him the keys of the kingdom

Statues of the Sacred Heart of Jesus show

....

....

....

Exam support

You might be asked to evaluate a statement such as: *'You need statues and sculptures to help you be a good Christian.'* This table might help answer such a question:

Arguments for	Arguments against
To be a good Christian you need to love God and love your neighbour. Statues help you do this because: ● statues of the Sacred Heart help Christians adore and thank God for his love ● crucifixes help Christians to love God for the sacrifice he made on the cross for their sins ● statues of the Virgin Mary help Christians pray for her help for problems their neighbours may be facing ● statues of the saints help Christians pray for the saints' help in curing the problems of the world.	● Protestants believe statues stop you being a good Christian because they break the second of the ten commandments. ● You can love God by going to Mass regularly, which does not need statues. ● You can love God by taking the other sacraments, none of which requires statues. ● You can love your neighbour by working for CAFOD which does not require statues.

Topic 1.4.5 The meaning and significance of sculptures and statues

Topic 1.4.6 The purpose and use of symbolism and imagery in religious art

Symbolism means using an object or a word to represent an abstract idea. A symbol contains a wealth of meaning – for example, red on a traffic light is a sign to stop, but red is a symbol of danger, evil and death.

Religious symbols are used to communicate the underlying message of a religion to make its meaning more accessible to people, but in pointing to the holy it comes to represent the holy, so religious symbols have a certain holiness in themselves.

Christianity is full of symbols, which express Catholic beliefs:
- The cross can be a sign of Christianity, but it is also a symbol of divine love and forgiveness, of Jesus' sacrifice on the cross.
- The crucifix is a representation of Jesus on the cross, which symbolises the Passion of Christ, a symbol of his death for the sins of the world.
- A fish is used to symbolise Christianity as fish regularly featured in the Gospels and some of the first disciples were fishermen. Also, the Greek for fish formed the first letters of 'Jesus Christ, Son of God, Saviour', making it a symbol, pointing to deeper truths of Christianity.
- The **Chi-Rho** is a symbol made from the first two letters of 'Christ' in Greek with a circle through it to symbolise that Christ has risen from the dead.
- The dove symbolises the Holy Spirit as seen in Christ's baptism.
- Eagles are symbols in the Bible of the power and speed of God's message based on the prophet Isaiah's claim that those who wait on the Lord will rise up with wings like eagles.
- The Alpha and Omega letters of the Greek alphabet are a symbol of Jesus. These are the first and the last letters of the Greek alphabet and symbolise the eternal nature of Christ. Jesus described himself as the first and the last in Revelation.

> **Alpha** The first letter of the Greek alphabet.
>
> **Chi-Rho** A symbol using the first two Greek letters (ch and r) in Christ.
>
> **Evangelist** Author of a Gospel.
>
> **Omega** The last letter of the Greek alphabet.
>
> **Paschal** Relating to Easter.

The four evangelists have their own symbols, each with wings to symbolise their role as messengers:
- Matthew's symbol is a winged man spreading the Gospel as his Gospel stresses the Incarnation of Jesus – God made man.
- Mark's symbol is a winged lion as his Gospel shows Jesus as a courageous, miracle-working figure – a lion.
- Luke's symbol is a winged ox as his Gospel stresses the sacrifice of Jesus and oxen were often offered as sacrifices.
- John's symbol is a winged eagle. The soaring eagle suggests God's word as his Gospel speaks of Jesus as the Word of God made man.

Many of these symbols will be found in a Catholic church, especially the cross and the crucifix. Some churches have sculptures of an eagle on the lectern. The **Alpha** and the **Omega** might be on church vestments and are always on the **Paschal**, or Easter candle.

Sources of wisdom and authority

Isaiah 45 says that those who wait for the Lord shall renew their strength, and mount up with wings like eagles.

According to Revelation chapter 1, Jesus said, 'It is I, the First and the Last. I am alive for ever and ever.'

Now test yourself

1 Evangelist means:
   (a) The first letter of the Greek alphabet
   (b) The author of a Gospel
   (c) The last letter of the Greek alphabet
   (d) Relating to Easter
2 Alpha is:
   (a) The first letter of the Greek alphabet
   (b) The author of a Gospel
   (c) The last letter of the Greek alphabet
   (d) Relating to Easter
3 Paschal means:
   (a) The first letter of the Greek alphabet
   (b) The author of a Gospel
   (c) The last letter of the Greek alphabet
   (d) Relating to Easter
4 Omega is:
   (a) The first letter of the Greek alphabet
   (b) The author of a Gospel
   (c) The last letter of the Greek alphabet
   (d) Relating to Easter

Activities

Complete the answers to these questions:

1 Outline **three** Catholic symbols.

The cross is a symbol of divine love and forgiveness. The crucifix is a representation of Jesus on the cross, which symbolises the Passion of Christ. Another symbol is

....

....

2 Explain **two** reasons why the symbol of the Alpha and Omega is important for Catholics. In your answer you must refer to a source of wisdom and authority.

The Alpha and the Omega letters of the Greek alphabet are a symbol of Jesus. These are the first and the last letters of the Greek alphabet and are important for Catholics because they symbolise the eternal nature of Christ. As Jesus said in Revelation, 'It is I, the first and the last. I am alive for ever and ever.'

Another reason they are important is because they can be found on

....

....

....

Exam support

You might be asked to evaluate a statement such as: *'Catholic symbols only have meaning for Catholics.'* This table might help answer such a question:

Arguments for	Arguments against
• The crucifix is a representation of Jesus on the cross, which symbolises the Passion of Christ, something only Catholics understand. • A fish is used to symbolise Christianity but only Catholics would understand that the Greek for fish formed from the first letters of 'Jesus Christ, Son of God, Saviour'. • The Chi-Rho is a symbol and only Catholics would understand it is made from the first two letters of 'Christ' in Greek with a circle through it to symbolise that Christ has risen from the dead. • Only Catholics would understand that the Alpha and Omega symbol stands for Jesus being the first and the last.	• The crucifix is used by other Christians and even non-Christians understand the Passion of Christ even if they don't believe it. • The fish is used as a sign of being a Christian by lots of Protestant Christians who wear it as a lapel badge. • The Chi-Rho symbol appears in lots of non-Catholic Christian churches, so they must understand it. • The Alpha and Omega is a major symbol for many non-Catholic Christians.

Topic 1.4.7 The meaning and significance of drama, mystery plays and passion plays

Drama can be defined as an exciting, emotional or unexpected event and is usually connected with theatre or television plays, or with films. Christianity is based on a drama, the drama of the Passion, and the Bible is full of drama. Consequently, in the days before most people could read, Christianity relied on drama to put across its message.

Mystery plays were **medieval** dramas produced by travelling actors and the local town guilds. These plays tried to put across the message of Christianity (creation and the Fall, the nativity and baptism of Jesus, the Passion, the resurrection, the **assumption** and **coronation of Mary**) by:
- being in the language of the people, not Latin
- using humour, including slapstick
- putting real-life situations into the plots so that people could empathise
- making the spiritual message clear and simple.

The plays were very popular and so were an effective teaching tool for the Church. The York and Chester plays have been revived and are performed regularly.

Passion plays are produced by Christians throughout the world, especially in South and Central America, the Philippines and Catholic countries in Europe, the most famous being produced every ten years in Oberammergau in Bavaria. These plays tell the story of Jesus' last days, from Palm Sunday to the cross, and end with the resurrection. They are usually performed by local actors and try to put across the message of Christ's Passion (forgiveness, **atonement**, eternal life, God's love) by:
- being in the language of the people
- bringing the drama of the events to life
- making the Passion a spectacle (there are often at least 500 actors)
- putting in some ordinary events to make the events relevant to people's lives.

The way drama is used to express belief in church and other settings

- Mystery plays express Catholic beliefs about creation, the fall of man, the Incarnation, the Last Supper, the Atonement, the crucifixion, the Blessed Virgin Mary. They bring the beliefs to life though play and characterisation.
- The Mass is a drama when the priest(s) re-enacts Christ's sacrifice and the Last Supper in the Eucharistic prayer to express Catholic beliefs about transubstantiation and atonement.
- Catholic beliefs about the Passion and the resurrection are expressed in the dramatic events of passion plays.
- In the Easter liturgy, the Gospel of the Passion is broken down into many voices for the different characters, so presenting Catholic beliefs about the Passion through dramatic readings.
- At the **Veneration of the Cross**, the people take part in the drama as they express their beliefs about Christ's sacrifice by filing up to kiss the cross.
- At the Easter vigil on Holy Saturday, the Paschal candle is lit from the new fire of Easter, expressing Catholic belief in the resurrection as the light of the resurrected Christ, and is brought into the darkened church.

Assumption The belief that the Virgin Mary was taken into heaven body and soul.

Atonement Reconciliation between God and humans.

Coronation of Mary The Virgin Mary being declared and appointed Queen of Heaven.

Medieval To do with the Middle Ages.

Veneration of the Cross Kissing and honouring a cross, especially on Good Friday.

Sources of wisdom and authority

The Catechism teaches that God has gradually revealed himself to the world just like a drama which unfolds throughout the whole history of salvation.

Now test yourself

1 The belief that the Virgin Mary was taken into heaven body and soul is called the:
(a) Immaculate conception
(b) Assumption
(c) Atonement
(d) Medieval

2 Reconciliation between God and humans is known as the:
(a) Immaculate conception
(b) Assumption
(c) Atonement
(d) Medieval

3 Anything to do with the Middle Ages is called:
(a) Immaculate conception
(b) Assumption
(c) Atonement
(d) Medieval

4 Kissing and honouring a cross is called:
(a) Adoration of the cross
(b) Beatification of the cross
(c) Veneration of the cross
(d) Sanctification of the cross

Activities

Complete the answers to these questions:

1 Outline **three** ways in which mystery plays express Catholic beliefs.

One way mystery plays express Catholic beliefs is by using the language of the people, not Latin. Another way is by putting real-life situations into the plots so that people can empathise. A third way is

....

....

2 Explain **two** ways in which drama expresses Catholic beliefs. In your answer you must refer to a source of wisdom and authority.

One way is in the drama of the Mass, when the priest(s) re-enacts Christ's sacrifice and the Last Supper in the Eucharistic prayer to express Catholic beliefs about transubstantiation and atonement through the drama of the Mass.

The Catechism teaches that God has gradually revealed himself to the world just like a drama which unfolds throughout the whole history of salvation.

Another way in which drama expresses Catholic beliefs is

....

....

Exam support

You might be asked to evaluate a statement such as: *'Mystery plays are just a mystery to most people.'* This table might help answer such a question:

Arguments for	Arguments against
Mystery plays try to put across the message of the Fall, the nativity, the Passion, the resurrection, the assumption of Mary but don't explain: ● why God allowed Adam and Eve to sin at the Fall ● how God could become a man and still be God, controlling the universe ● how God the infinite being could die ● how Mary could be taken into heaven.	Mystery plays make Catholic beliefs easier to understand because they: ● are in the language of the people, not Latin ● use humour, including slapstick ● put real-life situations into the plots so that people can empathise ● make the spiritual message very clear and simple.

Topic 1.4.8 The nature and use of traditional and contemporary styles of music in worship

REVISED

The Catholic Church believes that music and song are an appropriate response to the wonder of God's love seen in the coming of Christ. Indeed, music has been used to praise God from the earliest days of the Bible – the Psalms are hymns and they have many references to the use of musical instruments to praise God.

The Catechism talks about the early Christians composing hymns and **canticles** (songs) about the work of Christ and praises of God (**doxology**) for the wonderful salvation brought about by Christ.

Some of the great composers have written church music – consider Mozart's Great Mass and Requiem Mass, Beethoven's *Missa solemnis* and Andrew Lloyd Webber's Requiem. The main types of music used in ordinary worship are:

- **Hymns –** hymn means song of praise. Hymns have been sung for thousands of years and can be found in many religions. Catholic hymns are often addressed to God and express beliefs and emotions. The most famous were written in Victorian times, for example 'Faith of our Fathers', 'Stabat Mater', 'Hail Holy Queen', though Catholics also sing Protestant hymns such as 'Amazing Grace'. Modern hymns have been composed in a more contemporary style, such as 'Here I am Lord', 'One Bread One Body', and these are more popular in modern Catholic worship.
- **Plainchant –** the early Christians developed a tradition of unaccompanied singing from Jewish synagogue worship. There are two types: **responsorial** and **antiphonal** chant. After Vatican II introduced the New Rite Mass, the use of plainsong declined and is now mainly restricted to the monastic orders.
- **Psalms** are sacred songs or hymns contained in the biblical Book of Psalms. They have been used in Jewish worship since they were written in about 1000BCE by King David who was a harpist, and so they were probably for both voices and instruments. There are psalms of praise, thanksgiving and lament, and so they contain many human emotions about life, God and religion, which makes them still relevant for worship today.
- **Worship songs** are short hymns with only one or two verses. They put a Bible verse or simple Christian message to contemporary music using guitar and/or keyboards. They can be lively praise songs with dance moves or calmer adoration, many of which developed from Youth 2000, which was a response to Pope John Paul II's call to young people to evangelise each other to celebrate the new millennium. As a result, many Catholic churches now have worship songs incorporated into the Mass.

Different ways in which music may be used

- Music will open the Mass as the priest and servers enter.
- Important parts of the Mass, for example the Gloria, the Gospel Acclamation and parts of the Eucharistic Prayer, are sung.
- Hymns and songs may feature in the Mass as the bread and the wine are brought to the altar.
- Contemplative music may feature in the Communion.

Antiphonal Plainchant where the verses are sung alternately by soloist and choir, or by choir and congregation.

Canticle A hymn or chant.

Doxology A praise of God.

Plainchant A style of unaccompanied singing for monastic offices or the Mass.

Responsorial Plainchant where a soloist or choir sings verse with a response from the choir or congregation.

Sources of wisdom and authority

Catechism 2641 says that the early Christians composed hymns and canticles to praise God for his work in the Incarnation, Passion, resurrection and ascension of his Son.

The Catechism also says that doxology, the praise of God, arises from God's marvellous work of salvation.

Psalm 150 teaches that people should praise the Lord with tambourine and dancing, with strings and flute and the clash of cymbals.

Now test yourself

1 Plainchant where the verses are sung alternately by soloist and choir or by choir and congregation is called:
   (a) Doxology
   (b) Responsorial
   (c) Antiphonal
   (d) Canticle

2 An old word for a hymn or chant is:
   (a) Doxology
   (b) Responsorial
   (c) Antiphonal
   (d) Canticle

3 Praise of God is called:
   (a) Doxology
   (b) Responsorial
   (c) Antiphonal
   (d) Canticle

4 Plainchant where a soloist or choir sings verse with a response from the choir or congregation is called:
   (a) Doxology
   (b) Responsorial
   (c) Antiphonal
   (d) Canticle

Activities

Complete the answers to these questions:

1 Outline **three** types of music used by Catholics in ordinary worship.

Hymns are songs of praise and have been sung for thousands of years. Another type of music is plainchant, which is unaccompanied singing developed from Jewish synagogue worship. A third type of music is

....

....

2 Explain **two** ways in which music is used to express belief in Catholicism. In your answer you must refer to a source of wisdom and authority.

Hymns use words and music to express beliefs and emotions to God, for example 'Hail Holy Queen' expresses Catholic beliefs about the Virgin Mary and 'One Bread One Body' expresses Catholic beliefs about the Eucharist. As the Catechism says, the early Christians composed hymns and canticles to praise God for his work in the Incarnation, the Passion, resurrection and ascension of his Son.

Another way is

....

....

Exam support

You might be asked to evaluate a statement such as: *'All music used in Catholic churches should be modern and lively.'* This table might help answer such a question:

Arguments for	Arguments against
• The music used in church should reflect the age in which we live. • The Church has a problem attracting and retaining young people and modern music makes church attractive to young people. • Music is an emotional gateway to God and so it needs to reflect the emotions of today. • Church music needs to show that church is for the modern world and is not stuck in the past.	• Many people find modern music does not promote a worshipful atmosphere. • People have different musical tastes and church music needs to reflect that difference, not just be modern. • Quieter, more traditional music is more likely to bring about feelings of worship and contemplation. • Traditional church music is a link to the past and helps worshippers realise the history they are part of.

2.1b Judaism – beliefs and teachings

Topic 2.1b.1 The nature of the Almighty

REVISED

The Jewish scriptures are known as the Tenakh from the three divisions of the Jewish scriptures: **Torah**, **Nevi'im** and **Ketuvim**.

The main Tenakh teachings about God are:

God is One. Judaism teaches strict monotheism. The basic teaching of the Torah is the *Shema*, which begins with the words, 'Hear O Israel, the Lord our God, the Lord is one.' The importance of this belief in God's oneness can be seen in the way:
- Jewish people have a **mezuzah** holding the *Shema* on their gates and doorframes
- Jewish men bind *tefillin* to their forehead and arm when they pray every morning
- Judaism teaches the unity of creation and the need for people to try to bring unity to society.

God is the Creator. The very first words of the Torah are, 'In the beginning God created the heaven and the earth.' God the Creator is the first of the Thirteen Principles of Faith set out by **Maimonides**. The Torah teaches that because God is the Creator, everything belongs to him. The universe and everything in it comes from God and therefore depends on God. Judaism teaches that God created the universe and his creation is good. In their prayer every day, Jewish people praise God who 'in His goodness renews the work of creation each day continually'. God's creation is good and so Jewish people care for the environment.

God the Law-giver. The **Tenakh** teaches that God is the great law-giver. He gave laws to help people look after the Earth in the way he wanted. God gave some laws to Noah and some to Abraham, but it was Moses who received all 613 commands (**Mitzvot**) of the Jewish law on Mount Sinai. Believing that God is the law-giver is important in Judaism today because God's laws (the Mitzvot) form the **halakhah**, which is the basis of how Jews live their lives today. The fact that God is a law-giver means that God cares about his creation and cares about humans.

God the Judge. The halakhah is the divine law of Judaism. It means 'the path that one walks'. Any divine law requires a divine judge and the Tenakh teaches that God is the divine judge who ensures that the good are rewarded and the evil are punished. Eventually God will make sure that justice reigns. The belief that God is judge is important for Jewish life today because it ensures that:
- the good are rewarded and the evil punished
- the world is protected from the chaos that would come if there was no way of making sure that people keep God's laws
- people know there will punishments for those who do not keep God's laws
- people know there will be rewards for those who do keep God's laws.

Halakhah The holy law of Judaism.

Ketuvim The books of the writings.

Maimonides Medieval rabbi and philosopher who wrote the Thirteen Principles.

Mezuzah A container for the *Shema* scroll put on doorposts.

Mitzvot Commandments/laws.

Nevi'im The books of the prophets.

Shema Statement of God's oneness.

Tefillin Leather container for *Shema* scroll to put on arms and head.

Tenakh The Jewish scriptures.

Torah The law book or books of Moses.

Sources of wisdom and authority

'Hear, O Israel! The Lord our God, the Lord is one.' Deuteronomy 6:4

'I believe with perfect faith that God is the Creator.' Thirteen Principles of the Faith.

Isaiah 33 says 'the Lord is our Law-Giver'

Psalm 9 says that God will judge the world in righteousness.

Now test yourself

1 The books of the writings are known as:
 (a) Torah
 (b) Ketuvim
 (c) Nevi'im
 (d) Mitzvot
2 The law book or books of Moses are known as:
 (a) Torah
 (b) Ketuvim
 (c) Nevi'im
 (d) Mitzvot

3 The Jewish scriptures are called:
 (a) Torah
 (b) Halakhah
 (c) Tenakh
 (d) Mitzvot
4 The holy law of Judaism is:
 (a) Torah
 (b) Halakhah
 (c) Tenakh
 (d) Mitzvot

Activities

Complete the answers to these questions:
1 Outline **three** Jewish beliefs about the nature of the Almighty.

Jews believe that the Almighty is one, there is only one God. They also believe that the Almighty is

....

Another belief is

....

2 Explain **two** reasons why it is important for Jews that the Almighty is a law-giver. In your answer you must refer to a source of wisdom and authority.

Believing that God is the law-giver is important in Judaism today because God's laws (the Mitzvot) form the halakhah, which is the basis of how Jews live their lives today. Having the laws given by God means that Jews know exactly how they should live. As Isaiah says, God is our law-giver.

Another reason it is important that the Almighty is a law-giver is

....

....

....

Exam support

You might be asked to evaluate a statement such as: 'God's oneness is his most important characteristic.'
This table may help you answer such a question:

Arguments for	Arguments against
• It is the first belief mentioned in the *Shema*, which is the basis of Judaism. • The Thirteen Principles say, 'This God is One, not two or more than two, but One whose unity is different from all other unities that there are.' • It is because God is one that the creation is a unity. • Jews reminds themselves of God's unity many times a day as they touch a mezuzah.	• The most important part of a Jew's life is the halakhah, so perhaps being a law-giver is more important. • Most of the Torah is about the Mitzvot, so law-giving is most important. • The first of the Thirteen Principles is God the Creator, so perhaps that is more important. • Life would be chaotic if God was not the Judge who makes sure the good are rewarded and the evil are punished.

Topic 2.1b.2 *Shekhinah*

The Hebrew word *shekhinah* is deliberately difficult to define because it is a way of describing the Almighty's presence in the world. Attempting to use finite words to describe the infinite cannot be accurate.

Shekhinah means 'the majestic presence of God' or 'the glory of God'. The **rabbis** always used the term *shekhinah* for any form of human contact with God because humans can have contact only with that part of God on Earth, not God's immensity.

The Torah speaks of:
- God's presence (*shekhinah*) going with Moses to guide him through the wilderness to the promised land
- the *shekhinah* as cloud and smoke on Mount Sinai when God gave the commandments
- Moses' face shining when he came into contact with the divine presence
- God choosing the **tabernacle** as the place for his presence which is so holy that nothing unclean can touch it.

The other books of the Tenakh speak of the prophets having visions of the presence of God, and the writings of later rabbis who use *shekhinah* for the presence of God in the world.

> **Kabbalah** Jewish mysticism.
>
> **Mount Zion** The holy hill in Jerusalem where the Temple was.
>
> **Rabbi** An ordained Jewish religious leader/teacher.
>
> **Tabernacle** The holy place containing the Ark of the Covenant.
>
> **Temple** The centre of worship built by Solomon in Jerusalem and destroyed in 70CE.

Different understanding of *shekhinah* for Jews today

- Some Reform Jews base themselves on the teachings of Maimonides, who described the *shekhinah* as a light created to be a link between God and the world.
- Others regard the *shekhinah* as an expression for the various ways in which God is related to the world.
- Others believe that *shekhinah* simply means God. They feel that *shekhinah* and God are interchangeable words.
- In the **kabbalah** (Jewish mysticism), *shekhinah* is the gateway to higher consciousness, which brings followers into God's presence.

Shekhinah is important for Judaism because:
- the idea of *shekhinah* shows that, however close Jews may feel to God, God's presence is so holy and awesome that it must be respected, which is why Jews only use God's complete name in worship
- the *shekhinah* being at the **Temple**, **Mount Zion** and Jerusalem is what makes those places so special for some Jews *'I saw the Lord seated on a throne, high and exalted and the rain of his robe filled the Temp Isaio 6:1'*
- the teaching that Moses was surrounded by the *shekhinah* when he received the Torah means that Moses received the Mitzvot directly from God, so they are God's words
- the *shekhinah* means God's presence is in the world and believers might come across the *shekhinah* at any time.

Different understandings of the word *shekhinah*

- *Shekhinah* shows that God is far beyond human thought and so there are many ways of understanding his presence.
- *Shekhinah* allows Judaism to relate God to modern theological debates about whether God is masculine.
- *Shekhinah* makes it easier for Jews and Christians to come together in their search for God.

The concept of *shekhinah* in the kabbalah brought together different religions, making it easier to break down religious hatred – there are Christian, Sunni Muslim and Shi'ah Muslim kabbalists.

Sources of wisdom and authority

Exodus 33 says 'My presence will go with you and I will give you rest'.

Exodus 19 says that 'Mount Sinai was covered with smoke, because the Lord descended on it in fire.'

'I saw the Lord seated on a throne, high and exalted and the rain of his robe filled the Temple.' Isaiah 6:1.

Now test yourself

1 Mount Zion refers to:
   (a) Jewish mysticism
   (b) The holy hill in Jerusalem on which the Temple stood
   (c) An ordained Jewish religious leader/teacher
   (d) The holy place containing the Ark of the Covenant
2 Rabbi refers to:
   (a) Jewish mysticism
   (b) The holy hill in Jerusalem on which the Temple stood
   (c) An ordained Jewish religious leader/teacher
   (d) The holy place containing the Ark of the Covenant
3 Tabernacle refers to:
   (a) Jewish mysticism
   (b) The holy hill in Jerusalem on which the Temple stood
   (c) An ordained Jewish religious leader/teacher
   (d) The holy place containing the Ark of the Covenant

Activities

Complete the answers to these questions:

1 Outline **three** different Jewish understandings of *shekhinah*.

Some modern Jews base themselves on the teachings of Maimonides, who described the shekhinah as a light created to be a link between God and the world. Others regard the shekhinah as an expression for the various ways in which God is related to the world. Others understand it as

....

....

2 Explain **two** reasons why *shekhinah* is important for Jews today. In your answer you must refer to a source of wisdom and authority.

Shekhinah is important for Jews today because the idea of shekhinah shows that however close Jews may feel to God, God's presence is so holy and awesome that they must always have a deep sense of respect for God. This sense of respect is shown by Jews only referring to God's names in worship.

The Tenakh describing the shekhinah as being at the Temple, Mount Zion and Jerusalem is what makes those places so special for many Jews. As Isaiah said,

....

....

Exam support

You might be asked to evaluate a statement such as: *'The concept of* shekhinah *is not important for understanding Judaism.'* This table may help you answer such a question:

Arguments for	Arguments against
You don't need to understand *shekhinah* to understand the main features of Judaism: ● That there is only one God. ● That God chose the people of Israel to be his people in his covenants with Moses and Abraham. ● That God gave the Mitzvot as a way of life for the Jewish people. ● That God will send the Messiah to establish his kingdom.	*Shekhinah* shows the major Jewish beliefs: ● That God's reality is far beyond anything humans can even think of. ● That God is absolutely holy and must not be defiled by humans. ● That God's *shekhinah* with Moses proves Moses received the Mitzvot directly from God. ● That their special connections with God's *shekhinah* make Jerusalem and the Temple special and holy.

Topic 2.1b.3 Messiah

The word Messiah means 'anointed one' and was used to refer to the kings of Israel who were anointed. When the Israelite kingdom was captured by the Babylonians and the monarchy ended (586 BCE), the Messiah became a religious ideal.

The purpose of the Messiah

Jews believe the Messiah will:
● rebuild the Temple in Jerusalem
● unite all the peoples of the world
● make all the peoples of the world aware of the presence of God
● bring in the **Messianic Age** when all will live at peace.

The nature of the Messiah

Most Jews believe that the Messiah will be:
● a descendant of King David
● a human, not a divine being
● a man of great piety and close to God.

The Messiah in the scriptures

There are no references to the Messiah in the Torah, but the Nevi'im say that the Messiah will be a descendant of David, will rule wisely and justly, will ensure the poor are treated fairly and will rebuild the Temple in Jerusalem.

Messianic Age

The time when the Messiah comes is known as the Messianic Age or *Olam Ha-Ba*. The Nevi'im say that during this time there will be peace among all nations and all the Jewish people will return to Israel, the Temple will be rebuilt, and the whole world will accept God and Judaism.

Different understandings of the Messiah

● Some Orthodox rabbis taught that the Messiah will not come until all Jewish people observe all the Mitzvot fully.
● Some Jewish rabbis have believed they know when the Messiah will arrive. This is particularly so among **Ultra-Orthodox** Jewish groups.
● Most Orthodox rabbis have followed the teaching of Maimonides that no one can know when the Messiah will come other than God himself.
● Many Reform Jews no longer believe in the idea of an individual Messiah who will make the world perfect. They believe it is up to individual Jewish people to change this world, bringing the nations together and establishing justice and peace just as the Tenakh predicts.

Belief in the coming of the Messiah is important for Jews because:
● it is one of the Thirteen Principles of the Faith
● Jews pray for the coming of the Messiah, the return of those who were forced to leave at the **Exile**, reward to the righteous, the rebuilding of Jerusalem and the restoration of the Temple service three times a day.

These different Jewish ideas about the Messiah mean it is possible to be a good Jew without supporting the destruction of Palestine because **Zionism** and Judaism are not the same.

Exile When the Jewish people had to leave their homeland and live elsewhere.

Messianic Age A time when all nations will live at peace and there will be justice in the world.

Olam Ha-Ba The world to come.

Ultra-Orthodox The very Orthodox like the Hasidic and the Haredi.

Zionism The belief that the boundaries of the old Kingdom of Israel should be those of the modern Jewish homeland.

Sources of wisdom and authority

The prophet Jeremiah prophesied the Messiah being a descendant of David who will rule wisely.

'I believe with perfect faith in the coming of the Messiah. However long it takes, I will await His coming every day.' (Thirteen Principles No. 12.)

Now test yourself

1 When the Jewish people had to leave their homeland and live elsewhere it was known as the:
   (a) Exodus
   (b) Passover
   (c) Exile
   (d) Exeunt

2 *Olam Ha-Ba* means:
   (a) The Messianic Age
   (b) The world to come
   (c) Life after death
   (d) The final judgement

3 An example of Ultra-Orthodox Jews would be the:
   (a) Haroset
   (b) Hasidic
   (c) Huppah
   (d) Hechsher

4 The belief that the boundaries of the old Kingdom of Israel should be those of the modern Jewish homeland is:
   (a) Yeshivah
   (b) Zohar
   (c) Haredi
   (d) Zionism

Activities

Complete the answers to these questions:

1 Outline **three** Jewish beliefs about the nature of the Messiah.

Jews believe that the Messiah will be a descendant of King David. They also believe the Messiah will be a human, not a divine being. Another belief is that the Messiah will be

a man of great piety and close to God

2 Explain **two** reasons why beliefs about the Messiah are important for Jews today. In your answer you must refer to a source of wisdom and authority.

Beliefs about the Messiah are important for Jews today because belief in the Messiah is one of the Thirteen Principles of the Faith. It is Principle 12, which says, 'I believe with perfect faith in the coming of the Messiah.' All Jews should believe the Thirteen Principles so belief in the Messiah must be important.

Also Jews pray

for the coming of the Messiah, the return of those who were forced to leave at the Exile.

Exam support

You might be asked to evaluate a statement such as: *'All Jews should have the same beliefs about the Messiah.'* This table may help you answer such a question:

Arguments for	Arguments against
• The Thirteen Principles say all Jews must believe in the Messiah so they should have the same beliefs.	• Maimonides said no one knows when the Messiah will come so there are bound to be different opinions.
• The Tenakh tells Jews about the Messiah and all Jews should believe the Tenakh.	• There is nothing in the Torah and not a lot in the rest of the Tenakh so Jews are bound to elaborate the beliefs.
• If Jews don't have the same beliefs, non-Jews might not believe them.	• Judaism is a religion which has always had different beliefs, for example Orthodox and Reform.
• If belief in the Messiah is true, then they should all have the same belief.	• There are so many different interpretations of the Mitzvot which are clearly written so there are bound to be different interpretations of such a vague belief as the Messiah.

Topic 2.1b.4 The covenant at Sinai

The nature and history of the covenant at Sinai

Moses led the Jewish people out of captivity in Egypt (the **Exodus**) and then spent 40 years wandering in the Sinai wilderness preparing the people to enter and possess the Promised Land. It was during this time that God appeared to Moses on Mount Sinai to make the **covenant**. A covenant is a binding agreement between two parties with certain conditions and promises.

The covenant at Sinai (known as the Mosaic Covenant):
- was an agreement between God and the Jewish people
- was written on two tablets of stone kept in the **Ark of the Covenant** stored in the tabernacle and later the Temple
- stated that if the people kept the 613 laws given to Moses on Sinai, they would be God's special people.

The Mosaic Covenant is important for Jews today because:
- the 613 Mitzvot given by God on Sinai provide the way of life for Jewish people and separate them from **Gentiles**
- it means that Jewish people have a duty to keep the Mitzvot as part of their side of the covenant to make them God's people
- the Tenakh teaches that by keeping the Mosaic Covenant, the Jewish people will fulfil their destiny of bringing the whole world to worship God
- the laws given to Moses are so important for modern Jews that the divisions into Reform and Orthodox, Ultra-Orthodox, etc. are all based on interpretations of how Jewish people should obey the Mosaic Covenant.

The Ten Commandments (Decalogue)

Although Moses was given 613 commandments from God, Jews regard the Ten Commandments (**decalogue**) as special because they are commandments to be kept by all Jews, women as well as men, children as well as adults. These commands are particularly important to Jews for several reasons:
- Jewish people remind themselves that they worship one God only (first commandment) every time they touch the mezuzah and three times a day in the prayers.
- The second commandment means Jewish people ban any form of statue from the synagogue and their home and argue about what art is permitted in Judaism, showing how seriously the second commandment is taken.
- The third commandment means Jewish people do not use God's name in any form of swearing and say 'the Almighty' or '**Hashem**' rather than speaking the word God.
- The fourth commandment means Orthodox Jews do no work on *Shabbat*, which begins at sunset on Friday and ends when the stars appear on Saturday.
- The fifth commandment helps Jewish people in their family life and parents in their task of bringing up their children to be good Jews.
- The last five commandments are very important when making moral decisions as they give clear moral guidance: do not steal, do not kill, do not commit adultery, do not lie and do not desire other people's things.

Applying the Ten Commandments means Jewish people should act against all forms of greed and materialism.

Ark of the Covenant The holy container for the tablets of the commandments.

Covenant An agreement between two parties.

Decalogue The Ten Commandments.

Exodus The Israelites' escape from slavery in Egypt.

Gentiles Non-Jews.

Hashem The Name, a word used to refer to God without mentioning his name.

Shabbat The Jewish holy day, Saturday, the seventh day of the week.

Sources of wisdom and authority

Deuteronomy records Moses entering into a covenant with God making God the God of Israel and Israel God's people.

The Ten Commandments in Exodus 20 are:
1 You shall have no other gods before me.
2 Do not make idols.
3 Do not misuse the name of the Lord your God.
4 Remember the Sabbath day to keep it holy.
5 Honour your father and your mother.
6 Do not murder.
7 Do not commit adultery.
8 Do not steal.
9 Do not bear false testimony.
10 Do not covet other people's possessions.

Now test yourself

1 An agreement between two parties is known as a:
 (a) Decalogue
 (b) Hashem
 (c) *Shabbat*
 (d) Covenant

2 The Ten Commandments are also known as the:
 (a) Decalogue
 (b) Hashem
 (c) *Shabbat*
 (d) Covenant

3 A word used to refer to God without mentioning his name is:
 (a) Decalogue
 (b) Hashem
 (c) *Shabbat*
 (d) Covenant

4 The seventh day of the week is known in Judaism as:
 (a) Decalogue
 (b) Hashem
 (c) *Shabbat*
 (d) Covenant

Activities

Complete the answers to these questions:

1 Outline **three** of the Ten Commandments.

One commandment is 'You shall have no other gods before me'. Another commandment is 'Do not make for yourself an idol'. And a third is

....

2 Explain **two** ways in which Moses is important for Jewish people. In your answer you must refer to a source of wisdom and authority.

Moses is important for Jewish people because he received the covenant on Mount Sinai when God promised to be the God of the Jewish people if they agreed to keep his laws expressed in the 613 Mitzvot. Deuteronomy records Moses entering into a covenant with God making God the God of Israel and Israel God's people.

Another reason is

....
....
....

Exam support

You might be asked to evaluate a statement such as: *'The Mosaic Covenant is not relevant for Jewish life today.'* This table may help you answer such a question:

Arguments for	Arguments against
● Reform Jews believe the 613 Mitzvot are not God's words since the Torah was written by humans inspired by God. ● They feel it is the moral commands of the law which must be followed rather than the details of the halakhah such as keeping kosher, which are irrelevant and do not fit with modern life. ● They think the attitude to women in the Mitzvot is totally sexist and should be rejected; women should be treated completely equally. ● They think the *Shabbat* rules in the Mitzvot are irrelevant to modern life and that *Shabbat* can be kept special without rejecting life in the modern world.	● Orthodox Jews feel the covenant is totally relevant and they live their lives following the halakhah. ● They believe that following the details of halakhah such as keeping kosher is quite compatible with living in the modern world. ● They think it is possible to treat women as equals in life while giving them separate roles and practices in religion. ● They feel that keeping the details of *Shabbat* and kosher help to remind them of their heritage as God's people and to show their devotion to God.

Topic 2.1b.5 The covenant with Abraham

A thousand years before Moses, the Torah says that God called Abraham to leave his family in Iraq and travel to **Canaan** (Palestine) to worship the one true God.

The Abrahamic Covenant

God's side of the covenant was his promise to make a great nation from Abraham's son and to give the land of Canaan to Abraham's descendants as 'an everlasting possession'. Abraham's side of the agreement was for Abraham and every male descendant to be circumcised and for Abraham and his family to worship God alone.

As a result of the covenant, Jewish males are circumcised and Jewish people worship God alone. However, some liberal Reform Jews feel it is the Mosaic Covenant that is important for Jewish people, not the Abrahamic one, and they do not circumcise their children.

Abraham's grandson, Jacob, was renamed Israel by God and his 12 sons became the children of Israel and inherited Abraham's promise. Any **ethnic Jew** is descended from these 12 and has a right to be a citizen of the state of Israel whether he or she follows the religion or not.

The Abrahamic Covenant is important for Jews today:
- Most Jewish baby boys are circumcised, usually at eight days old, and enter into the covenant of Abraham (**Brit Milah**).
- The **Brit Chayim** (covenant of life) ceremony for Jewish baby girls among Reform and Liberal Jews welcomes girls into the Jewish faith and claims them as an heir to the Abrahamic Covenant.
- The covenant gave rise to the idea that Jewish people had a right to live in the area that was the ancient Kingdom of Israel, which has led to the importance of the land of Israel to Jewish people. The state of Israel was established in 1947 as a place of security for all Jews and Jewish people living anywhere in the world have the right to live in Israel and become a citizen.
- The state of Israel has been recognised by the United Nations since 1947 but has never been recognised by the Palestinians. Consequently, another major effect of the idea of the Children of Israel has been the conflict between Israel and the Palestinian people, and Arab states, in the Middle East.

There is a major debate in the Jewish communities outside Israel about the idea of the state of Israel being a fulfilment of God's promise to Abraham to give the Children of Israel the Promised Land. Ultra-Orthodox groups outside Israel teach that the return to the Promised Land will come only with the coming of the Messiah and that rather than supporting Israel, good Jews should be following all the Mitzvot and praying for the coming of the Messiah.

Brit Chayim Covenant of life ceremony for Reform girl babies.

Brit Milah Covenant of circumcision.

Canaan Ancient name for the land of Israel.

Ethnic Jew Someone who is Jewish through his or her genes rather than his or her religious belief.

Sources of wisdom and authority

God said to Abraham in Genesis, 'This land will be an everlasting possession to you and your descendants and I will be their God.'

God said to Abraham in Genesis, 'You are to undergo circumcision, and it will be the sign of the covenant between me and you.'

The Jewish Encyclopaedia says, 'Any child born of a Jewish mother is a Jew, whether circumcised or not.'

Now test yourself

1 The covenant of circumcision is known as:
   (a) Brit Milah
   (b) Brit Chayim
   (c) Canaan
   (d) Ethnic Jew
2 The covenant of life ceremony for Reform girl babies is known as:
   (a) Brit Milah
   (b) Brit Chayim
   (c) Canaan
   (d) Ethnic Jew
3 The ancient name for the land of Israel is:
   (a) Brit Milah
   (b) Brit Chayim
   (c) Canaan
   (d) Ethnic Jew
4 Someone who is Jewish through his or her genes rather than his or her religious belief is known as:
   (a) Brit Milah
   (b) Brit Chayim
   (c) Canaan
   (d) Ethnic Jew

Activity

Complete the answers to these questions:

1 Outline **three** features of the Abrahamic Covenant.

The Abrahamic Covenant said that the descendants of Abraham would become a great nation. It also said the Jewish people would occupy the Promised Land, and it said that all Jewish males

....

....

2 Explain **two** reasons why Jewish male babies are circumcised. In your answer you must refer to a source of wisdom and authority.

Jewish male babies are circumcised because God made a covenant with Abraham in which he promised to make a great nation from Abraham's son and to give the land of Canaan to Abraham's descendants as 'an everlasting possession', but only if Abraham and every male descendant was circumcised. As Genesis says,

....

....

Another reason is that circumcision is a mark in the flesh of being a member of the people of God. It is therefore a constant reminder for a Jewish man of his need to follow the halakhah and keep kashrut.

Exam support

You might be asked to evaluate a statement such as: 'The covenant with Moses is more important than the one with Abraham.' This table may help you answer such a question:

Arguments for	Arguments against
• Moses was given the 613 Mitzvot directly from God.	• Without Abraham there would be no Jews because God made him the father of Israel.
• The Mitzvot are the basis of the halakhah which is the Jewish way of life.	• Abraham was given the pledge of the Promised Land as the home for Jews.
• Moses was given the laws of *kashrut*, which mark out Jewish people from Gentiles.	• Abraham was given the covenant of circumcision which is the mark of all Jewish men.
• Moses was given the laws about the keeping of festivals such as Passover and Yom Kippur.	• Abraham's covenant was the first covenant and Abraham was the first to worship the one God.

Topic 2.1b.6 Sanctity of life

Judaism teaches that life is sacred – a gift from God. It follows that as God is the author of life, life itself is holy and must be valued and preserved. Judaism teaches that people should respect all human life – God is the Creator of life and so it is up to God alone to say when life will begin or end.

The sacredness and importance of human life is shown in the concept of *pikuach nefesh*. This means saving life and is the principle in Jewish law that the preservation of human life overrides almost all the other commandments in Judaism. The Talmud explains the principle of *pikuach nefesh* in Leviticus, which says, 'You shall therefore keep my statutes … which if a man do, he shall live by them' – the rabbis explain this as meaning that people live by the Mitzvot, not die by them. This means that even the Sabbath laws may be suspended to safeguard the health of the individual. A Jew is not merely permitted but is actually required to disregard a law that conflicts with treating a person whose illness may prove dangerous.

Pikuach nefesh **also comes from the Torah verse**, 'Do not do anything that endangers your neighbour's life' (Leviticus 19:16). According to *pikuach nefesh*, a person must do everything in their power to save the life of another, so it is permissible to break the Yom Kippur fast, break the **kashrut** rules, etc. The **Talmud** contains several instances where the laws of the Sabbath are to be broken to save the life of another, such as rescuing a child from the sea, breaking apart a wall that has collapsed on a child, breaking down a door about to close on an infant and extinguishing a fire.

Pikuach nefesh is based on the **sanctity of life** and shows the importance of this belief to Judaism.

Pikuach nefesh **is important for Jews today:**
- For Jews living in today's complex world, *pikuach nefesh* is a means of deciding when and where the Mitzvot take priority.
- Some Jews believe that abortion can never be allowed because of the sanctity of life, but *pikuach nefesh* means that if the mother's life is at risk, abortion must be allowed.
- Orthodox Judaism does not allow the use of condoms because the Torah teaches that the male seed is sacred, but the Jewish AIDS Trust promotes the use of condoms to prevent HIV transmission – this mitzvah can be broken to save the lives of people who may become infected with HIV.
- Orthodox Judaism does not allow transplant surgery because there is a mitzvah which says dead bodies must not be interfered with, but *pikuach nefesh* means this mitzvah can be broken to transplant on organ from a dead person to save a life.

> *Kashrut* Keeping Jewish food laws.
>
> *Pikuach nefesh* Saving a life, the principle that Mitzvot can be ignored to save life.
>
> **Sanctity of life** The belief that life is holy and belongs to God.
>
> **Talmud** Collection of Mishneh and other writings on the Jewish law.

Sources of wisdom and authority

Deuteronomy says, 'There is no God but me. I put to death and I bring to life.'

Leviticus says, 'You shall therefore keep my statutes … which if a man do, he shall live by them.'

Leviticus says, 'Do not do anything that endangers your neighbour's life.'

Now test yourself and Activities answers at www.hoddereducation.co.uk/myrevisionnotes

Now test yourself

1 Keeping Jewish food laws is called:
   (a) Mishneh
   (b) *Pikuach nefesh*
   (c) Talmud
   (d) *Kashrut*

2 The collection of Mishneh and other writings on the Jewish law is known as:
   (a) Nevi'im
   (b) *Pikuach nefesh*
   (c) Talmud
   (d) *Kashrut*

3 The principle that Mitzvot can be ignored to save life is:
   (a) Mishneh
   (b) *Pikuach nefesh*
   (c) Talmud
   (d) *Kashrut*

4 The collection of writings on the Jewish law is the:
   (a) Mishneh
   (b) *Pikuach nefesh*
   (c) Talmud
   (d) *Kashrut*

Activities

Complete the answers to these questions:

1 Outline **three** examples of *pikuach nefesh*.

One example would be driving someone who was very ill to hospital on Shabbat. Another would be allowing a blood transfusion even though Jews should not take blood. A third would be

....

....

2 Explain **two** reasons why Jews believe in the sanctity of life. In your answer you must refer to a source of wisdom and authority.

Jews believe in the sanctity of life because Judaism teaches that life is sacred since life is a gift from God. Leviticus says that Jews must not do anything which endangers the life of another, which implies that human life is sacred for Jewish people.

Another reason is because life was created by God and so only God has the right to end life. As God says in Deuteronomy,

....

....

Exam support

You might be asked to evaluate a statement such as: *'Orthodox Jews should always obey the Mitzvot.'* This table may help you answer such a question:

Arguments for	Arguments against
● Obeying the Mitzvot is part of the covenant at Sinai. ● Jews have to obey the Mitzvot as their part of the covenant; if not, they will no longer be God's people. ● Mitzvot are commandments from God and so must be obeyed. ● Nowhere in the Torah does it say the Mitzvot have to be obeyed only when Jews feel like it.	● The principle of *pikuach nefesh* says the Mitzvot may be broken if human life is at risk. ● The Talmud says the *Shabbat* Mitzvot can be broken to save a child's life. ● Jewish rabbis teach that the Mitzvot on blood can be broken for a blood transfusion. ● Rabbis say the Mitzvot on male seed can be broken to allow the use of condoms to prevent HIV.

Topic 2.1b.7 Moral principles and the Mitzvot

Moses received 613 **Mitzvot** on Mount Sinai. These are recorded in the Torah and the Jewish people are to observe them as their part of the Mosaic Covenant.

However, the Mitzvot in the Torah are stated only briefly and need some explanation:

- According to Jewish tradition, God gave this to Moses in the form of the 'Oral Torah', which was passed on by priests, judges and later rabbis.
- The oral and the written Torah made up the **halakhah**.
- The great rabbi Judah the Prince decided that the Oral Torah should be written down to prevent different forms of the halakhah developing in different areas. So he compiled the **Mishneh**.
- The rabbis' discussions on the Mishneh were written down in the Talmud.

For most Jewish people the Mitzvot and halakhah are one and the same thing because by following the halakhah they are keeping the Mitzvot.

Although the Mitzvot are commandments, each Jew must decide whether or not to follow them of their own free will. Judaism understands humans being made in God's image to mean that just as God is free to do whatever he wants, so humans have been created with free will: every person is free to choose whether to do good or evil. In particular they are free to choose whether to obey the Mitzvot or ignore them, which means it is something on which they can be judged.

It is important for Jewish people to understand the Mitzvot because:

- only if Jewish people really understands the Mitzvot will they keep them properly
- the Mitzvot are God's way of reaching out to humans, and keeping the Mitzvot is the way to develop a relationship with God
- understanding the Mitzvot leads to better relationships between people – for example, the laws about borrowing and lending teach compassion for those less well off than oneself
- some Mitzvot come with no given reason, for example on keeping **kosher**, and it is important to understand that these Mitzvot were given by God as a test of faith.

The Mitzvot are tremendously important for Orthodox Jews because they believe they are God's direct words to Moses and they cover the whole of life. For the Orthodox there is a right and a wrong way of doing everything: how to organise the kitchen, how to dress, what to eat, how to grow crops, whom Jewish people can marry, how to divorce, when Jewish people can work, which jobs they cannot do, etc.

The Mitzvot are not as important for Liberal Jews because they do not believe the Mitzvot came to Moses directly from God, so they believe that observing the Mitzvot is a matter of personal choice. For example, some Liberal Jews keep **kashrut**, some just eat kosher food, others ignore the food laws altogether.

Orthodox Jews believe the Mitzvot should be understood at a much deeper spiritual level. Mitzvah is closely related to the Hebrew word for 'connection' and Jewish people believe that the Mitzvot are a way for individuals to connect with God. By keeping the Mitzvot, Jewish people communicate with God, so becoming, in a true way, 'the People of God'.

Halakhah Jewish law from the written and Oral Torah.

Kashrut The state of being kosher.

Kosher Food which a Jew is allowed to eat.

Mishneh The Oral Torah.

Mitzvah Commandment (singular).

Mitzvot Commandments (plural).

Sources of wisdom and authority

Deuteronomy says that if the people keep God's commands and laws, they will live and increase, and the Lord God will bless them.

Deuteronomy says that choosing to obey the Mitzvot is a life or death choice.

The Talmud says, 'The Mitzvot were given for the purpose of refining people.'

Now test yourself

1 *Kashrut* means:
   (a) Jewish law from the written and Oral Torah
   (b) The state of being kosher
   (c) The Oral Torah
   (d) Commandment
2 Mishneh is:
   (a) Jewish law from the written and Oral Torah
   (b) The state of being kosher
   (c) The Oral Torah
   (d) Commandment
3 Mitzvah means:
   (a) Jewish law from the written and Oral Torah
   (b) The state of being kosher
   (c) The Oral Torah
   (d) Commandment

Activities

Complete the answer to this question:

1 Explain **two** different Jewish views about the Mitzvot. In your answer you must refer to a source of wisdom and authority.

Orthodox Jews believe the Mitzvot are God's direct words to Moses and they cover the whole of life. For the Orthodox there is a right and a wrong way of doing everything. The Mitzvot cover the whole of life and they are also the way to eternal life as they will be the basis of the final judgement. As Deuteronomy says, choosing to obey the Mitzvot is a life and death decision.

The Mitzvot are not as important for Reform/Liberal Jews because

....

....

....

Exam support

You might be asked to evaluate a statement such as: *'The Mitzvot are no longer relevant to modern life.'* This table may help you answer such a question:

Arguments for	Arguments against
• The Mitzvot were given in a totally different world and were relevant to that world, not this. • The Mitzvot treat women as second-class citizens who do not have to keep all the Mitzvot, which is not acceptable in today's world. • The Mitzvot on *kashrut* cannot be kept by Jews living outside a fairly large Jewish community. • The *Shabbat* Mitzvot don't fit with life in a multi-faith seven-day-week society.	• For the Orthodox they are God's words which will always be relevant. • The halakhah can be adapted according to different circumstances, keeping it relevant. • The *Shabbat* Mitzvot make Jews have a day of rest, which is very relevant to modern stressful life. • The rules of *kashrut* keep Jews on a healthy diet.

Topic 2.1b.8 Jewish beliefs about life after death

The Torah says the righteous will be reunited with their loved ones after death, 'being gathered to their people', that is there will be an afterlife which will involve meeting with dead family. **The rest of the Tenakh** says that God will end the world, raise the dead and create a new world by rebuilding Jerusalem and the Temple. God will decide what happens to people in the afterlife on the basis of how they have lived their lives and what they have believed.

However, there is disagreement about how these beliefs should be interpreted:
- **Most Jews believe in resurrection** because it is one of the **Thirteen Principles of Faith**. However, some believe the resurrection of the dead will occur during the Messianic era, others that it will follow the Messianic era. Some believe only the righteous will be resurrected, others that everyone will be resurrected.
- **Other rabbis have argued for the immortality of the soul**, the idea that the soul lives on after death as a spiritual being in *Olam Ha-Ba* (the spiritual world to come) where God dwells in what many think of as a parallel universe.

Different beliefs about the nature of judgement

- Some rabbis have taught that judgement will be based purely on behaviour – the good will go to heaven, the bad to Gehinnom (hell).
- **Maimonides** taught that all good people will go to heaven, even non-Jews – 'the pious of all the nations of the world have a portion in the world-to-come'.
- Others have suggested judgement will be based on a combination of belief and behaviour.
- Many modern rabbis prefer to concentrate on this life rather than worrying about the details of an afterlife about which no one can be certain.

Heaven and hell

The notion of heaven and hell has many different understandings:
- Many rabbis have taught that the souls of the totally righteous ascend to heaven (**Gan Eden**) whereas the souls of ordinary people go to the place of punishment (**Gehinnom**).
- Some rabbis have taught that Gehinnom is more like the Catholic purgatory and that souls are purified of their sins through punishment and fire.
- Some rabbis teach that totally evil souls are eternally damned and so are punished in Gehinnom for ever.
- Others teach that the souls of the truly wicked are destroyed by God and so cease to exist.

Belief in life after death is important for Jews today:
- It is the teaching of the Torah which Orthodox Jews believe is a direct communication from God that must be believed.
- It is the teaching of the other books of the Tenakh which Orthodox Jews believe are inspired by God.
- It is the teaching of the Talmud which most Jews try to follow.
- It is one of the Thirteen Principles of Faith which are the Jewish Creed.
- A life after death, in which people will be judged on how they live this life with the good rewarded and the evil punished, makes sense of this life.

Gan Eden Heaven.

Gehinnom Hell.

Maimonides Jewish scholar (1135–1204) who wrote the Mishneh Torah.

Olam Ha-Ba The spiritual world to come.

Thirteen Principles of Faith A summary of Jewish beliefs written by Maimonides.

Sources of wisdom and authority

Genesis says that Abraham breathed his last and he was gathered to his people.

Daniel says, 'Multitudes who sleep in the dust of the earth will awake, some to everlasting life.'

The Mishneh Torah says that 'The pious of all the nations of the world have a portion in the world-to-come.'

Now test yourself

1 The Jewish term for heaven is:
   (a) Gan Eden
   (b) Gehinnom
   (c) Halakhah
   (d) Maimonides
2 The scholar who wrote the Mishneh Torah was:
   (a) Gan Eden
   (b) Gehinnom
   (c) Halakhah
   (d) Maimonides

3 The Jewish term for hell is:
   (a) Gan Eden
   (b) Gehinnom
   (c) Halakhah
   (d) Maimonides
4 The code of Jewish law is called:
   (a) Gan Eden
   (b) Gehinnom
   (c) Halakhah
   (d) Maimonides

Activities

Complete the answers to these questions:

1 Outline **three** Jewish beliefs about resurrection.

Some Jews believe the resurrection will follow the Messianic Age. Others believe the resurrection will occur during the Messianic Age. Some believe

....

....

2 Explain **two** reasons why belief in life after death is important for Jews today. In your answer you must refer to a source of wisdom and authority.

Belief in life after death is important for some Jews today because it is the teaching of the Torah which Orthodox Jews believe is a direct communication from God which must be believed. When Genesis says that Abraham breathed his last and he was gathered to his people, it means that Abraham lived on after death.

Life after death is also the teaching of the other books of the Tenakh, such as Daniel, which says,

....

....

Exam support

You might be asked about the relationship between Christian and Jewish beliefs about life after death. This table should help answer such questions.

Similarities	Differences
• Both are split into Conservatives and Liberals — Conservative Jews have similar beliefs to Conservative Christians; Liberal Jews have similar beliefs to Liberal Christians. • Both Jews and Christians believe that this life is not all there is. • Both Jews and Christians believe there will be some sort of judgement after death based on how people have lived this life. • Both Jews and Christians believe that heaven is a place of paradise and that good people will go to heaven.	• Jews believe the Messiah will come at the Last Day, but Christians believe Jesus will return at the Last Day. • Most Jews believe that at the Last Day the Jewish people will bring the non-Jews to worship the Jewish God. • Conservative Jews have different beliefs from Liberal Christians (Liberal Christians do not believe in resurrection) and Liberal Jews have different beliefs from Conservative Christians (Liberal Jews do not believe in the Last Day).

2.2b Practices

REVISED

Public worship in Judaism has several purposes:

- To give a Jewish person a sense of belonging to a whole community of Jewish believers. *– opportunity to think about the meaning of life*
- To provide the opportunity to take part in those prayers which can only be said in a congregation.
- The **rabbis** taught that there is more merit in praying with a group than there is in praying alone.
- Public worship provides worship at statutory times and worshipping at set times gives order and purpose to people's religious life.

Features of Jewish public worship

- On *Shabbat* morning is the main service of the week when the **Sefer Torah** is taken out of the **Ark** and carried to the **bimah** for the rabbi to read the *sidra* and the rabbi gives a sermon.
- On *Shabbat* afternoon, synagogues have afternoon prayers when the Sefer Torah is again taken out of the Ark and a short part of the next week's *sidra* is read.
- Synagogues have special services for most of the festivals, especially Rosh Hashanah and **Yom Kippur** and **Simchat Torah**.

In Orthodox worship, prayers are said in Hebrew, men and women sit separately and some services are for men only, but in Liberal synagogues prayers are said in English, women attend all the services and sit with the men, and the rabbi may well be a woman.

Synagogue worship is important for the Jewish community because:

- to worship God with all your heart and all your soul requires people to be able to worship in community with other Jewish people
- synagogue worship is needed for the Jewish community to celebrate *Shabbat* properly
- synagogue worship gives the community the opportunity to share the great festivals and family celebrations.

Synagogue worship is important for a Jewish individual because:

- worshipping with others in the synagogue gives a sense of belonging to the Jewish community
- it gives the opportunity to think about the meaning of life
- sermons from the rabbi are the opportunity to discover more about what it means to be a Jew.

Why Jewish people worship in different ways

- Orthodox synagogues keep men and women separate because they believe the *Mitzvot* are God's words.
- Liberal/Reform synagogues demonstrate complete equality of the sexes because they believe the Torah was written by people inspired by God rather than being the direct word of God.

Ark Large cupboard at the front of the synagogue where the Torah scrolls are kept.

Bimah Raised platform in front of the Ark from which the scriptures are read.

Rabbi Spiritual leader of a Jewish community.

Rosh Hashanah Jewish New Year.

Sefer Torah The scroll of the Torah.

Shabbat The Sabbath (from sunset on Friday to sunset on Saturday).

Sidra The portion of the Torah read at *Shabbat* morning service.

Simchat Torah Festival celebrating the giving of the law.

Tallit Fringed garment worn by Orthodox Jews, especially for prayer.

Yom Kippur The Day of Atonement.

Sources of wisdom and authority

Psalm 116 says that worship is the way to repay God for his great goodness.

The prophet Zechariah said that men and women should be separated for periods of mourning.

The Talmud recommends men and women being separated for worship.

Now test yourself

1 The raised platform in front of the Ark from which the scriptures are read is called the:
   (a) *Sidra*
   (b) *Shabbat*
   (c) Rabbi
   (d) Bimah

2 The spiritual leader of a Jewish community is called a:
   (a) *Sidra*
   (b) *Shabbat*
   (c) Rabbi
   (d) Bimah

3 The time from sunset on Friday to sunset on Saturday is called:
   (a) *Sidra*
   (b) *Shabbat*
   (c) Rabbi
   (d) Bimah

4 The portion of the Torah read at *Shabbat* morning service is called:
   (a) *Sidra*
   (b) *Shabbat*
   (c) Rabbi
   (d) Bimah

Activities

Complete the answers to these questions:

1 Outline **three** purposes of public worship in Judaism.

One purpose of worship is to give a Jewish person a sense of belonging to a whole community of Jewish believers. Another purpose is to give the opportunity to think about the meaning of life. A third purpose is

[handwritten] to provide the opportunity to a whole community take part in those prayers which can only be said in congregation. sermons from the rabbi are the opportunity to discover more about what it means to a Jew.

2 Explain **two** reasons why Jewish people worship in different ways. In your answer you must refer to a source of wisdom and authority.

Orthodox Jews separate the sexes in worship and wear *tefillin* and *tallit* because this is commanded in the Mitzvot which they believe are the direct words of God given to Moses as described in Deuteronomy. Liberal/Reform Jews demonstrate complete equality of the sexes because they believe the Torah was written by people inspired by God rather than being the direct word of God.

Another reason is
....
....
....

Exam support

You might be asked to evaluate a statement such as: *'You can worship God just as well at home as in the synagogue.'* This table might help answer such a question:

Arguments for	Arguments against
• All the daily prayers can be said in the home because Orthodox women have to say them at home.	• *Shabbat* morning service should take place in the synagogue.
• Prayers have to be said in the home if there is not a *minyan* at synagogue.	• Some festivals such as Simchat Torah should take place in the synagogue.
• Some of the great festivals like the seder meal take place at home.	• Worshipping with others in the synagogue gives a sense of belonging to the Jewish community.
• God will accept people's worship wherever it takes place.	• Sermons from the rabbi give the opportunity to discover more about what it means to be a Jew.

Topic 2.2b.2 The Tenakh and Talmud

The Tenakh is the Jewish Bible. The name comes from the initial letters of **T**orah (the Five Books of Moses), **N**evi'im (the books of the prophets) and **K**etuvim (holy writings).

Torah contains 613 Mitzvot of Judaism and the history of the Jewish people from the creation to the Exodus and the death of Moses.

Nevi'im The history books, such as Joshua and Judges, and the books by prophets, such as Isaiah and Jeremiah, who believed they had a message from God to the people.

Ketuvim The writings are a mixture of history books (for example Esther), poetry books (for example Psalms), philosophical books (for example Job) and Daniel, a mix of history and prophecy. They express thoughts on the ultimate questions of life and morality.

The Tenakh is important because:

- the Psalms are an essential part of daily prayers and of much synagogue worship
- the Torah and Nevi'im are important in synagogue worship
- portions of the Ketuvim form an important part of some festivals
- Jewish people study and meditate on the books of the Tenakh to help their understanding of and their relationship with God.

The Talmud

Judaism teaches that when God gave Moses the Torah, he also gave him the Oral Torah to explain how the laws were to be obeyed. The written Torah and the Oral Torah together make up the halakhah. This was written down as the Mishneh by Rabbi Judah the Prince. This was studied by rabbis and their students and these discussions plus the Mishneh were written into the Talmud.

The Talmud is important because:
- it explains the meaning of the 613 Mitzvot
- it explains how the Mitzvot should be applied in the daily lives of Jews
- it is the basis of the **halakhah**, which is the foundation of Orthodox Jewish life today.

The nature and purpose of Jewish food laws

There are many Mitzvot about food, as a result of which Judaism developed quite complicated food laws known as kosher. This leads to the term *kashrut* (the state of being **kosher**) and *treifah* (not kosher). The main points are:
- Pigs, camels and shellfish must not be eaten.
- Animals must be slaughtered by the **shechitah** method of slitting the throat with a razor-sharp knife and draining out the blood.
- Kitchens should be in two halves, one for meat and one for dairy.

Keeping *kashrut* is very important for Orthodox Jews because:
- eating non-kosher foods, or not keeping a kosher kitchen, means breaking many of the Mitzvot
- it gives a sense of Jewish identity
- it gives a bond with fellow Jews
- it makes them think about God every time they decide to eat.

Keeping *kashrut* is not as important for Liberal Jews because they believe the laws of Moses are not God's direct commands.

Halakhah Jewish law.

Kashrut The state of being kosher.

Ketuvim Holy writings.

Kosher Fitting, food a Jew is permitted to eat.

Nevi'im The books of the prophets.

Shechitah Jewish method of slaughtering animals.

Torah The Five Books of Moses.

Treifah Not kosher.

Sources of wisdom and authority

'Anyone whose good deeds are more than his wisdom, his wisdom will endure. Anyone whose wisdom is more than his good deeds, his wisdom will not endure.' Saying from a first-century rabbi.

Leviticus says Jews should not eat animals which have a split hoof but do not chew the cud.

Deuteronomy says, 'Do not eat anything you find already dead.'

Leviticus says that before eating meat the blood must be drained out.

Deuteronomy says, 'Do not cook a young goat in its mother's milk.'

Deuteronomy says do not eat anything living in water that does not have fins and scales.

Now test yourself and Activities answers at **www.hoddereducation.co.uk/myrevisionnotes**

Now test yourself

1 The state of being kosher is called:
   (a) *Treifah*
   (b) *Kashrut*
   (c) Ketuvim
   (d) Nevi'im
2 The books of the writings are called:
   (a) *Treifah*
   (b) *Kashrut*
   (c) Ketuvim
   (d) Nevi'im

3 The books of the prophets are called:
   (a) *Treifah*
   (b) *Kashrut*
   (c) Ketuvim
   (d) Nevi'im
4 Anything that is not kosher is known as:
   (a) *Treifah*
   (b) *Kashrut*
   (c) Ketuvim
   (d) Nevi'im

Activities

Complete the answers to these questions:

1 Outline **three** foods that are not kosher.

One non-kosher food is fish without fins and scales. Another non-kosher food is animals with split hooves that do not chew the cud. A third non-kosher food is

....

2 Explain **two** reasons why the Talmud is important for Jews today. In your answer you must refer to a source of wisdom and authority.

One reason is because it explains the meaning of the 613 Mitzvot and Deuteronomy says that keeping the Mitzvot is what Jewish people must do to be part of the Mosaic Covenant.

Another reason is

....
....
....

Exam support

You might be asked to evaluate a statement such as: *'It's more important to get on well with people of other religions than to follow religious food laws which divide people.'* This table might help answer such a question:

Arguments for	Arguments against
• When religion divides people in a society it can lead to prejudice and discrimination. • Religious food laws divide society because people take offence if other people will not eat with them. • The great commandments are to love God and love your neighbour, and it is not loving your neighbour if you refuse to share a meal with them. • Failing to get on with people of other religions has led to the conflicts in Syria, Northern Ireland, etc.	• Orthodox Jews believe they must keep the Mitzvot because it is what God wants. • Eating non-kosher foods with non-Jews means breaking the Mitzvot. • Eating in a non-Jewish home which does not keep a kosher kitchen means breaking many of the Mitzvot. • Keeping the food laws gives a sense of Jewish identity and a bond with fellow Jews.

Topic 2.2b.3 Prayer

Prayer is an attempt by humans to communicate with God. In a sense, there are only two types of prayer: formal prayers, where a set form of prayer is used, and informal prayers, where a person makes up his or her own spontaneous prayer to express their feelings to God. The formal prayers of Judaism are contained in the Siddur (prayer book – there are different ones for the Orthodox and Reform) and are said in Hebrew by the Orthodox.

Jewish people believe **the purpose of prayer** is to:
- build up their relationship with God
- serve God with their heart, so obeying God's commandment: 'to love the Lord your God and to serve him with all your heart and with all your soul'
- take the opportunity to speak directly to God, knowing that God will listen and respond to prayers.

Much of Jewish worship and **prayer is centred on the home**. Some prayers at home are said as private prayers.
- When Jews wake up in the morning, they thank God for waking them before pouring water on their hands to purify themselves for the coming day.
- The day should end, as it should begin, by praising God by saying the *Shema*.
- The **mezuzah** on each door of the house is a constant reminder of God's presence – Jewish people touch the mezuzah and pray thanking God whenever they pass it.
- Jewish people pray and bless God before eating food and bless him again when they have finished eating.

A Jew should pray a set formal prayer three times a day: *shacharit* is morning prayer, *minchah* is afternoon prayer and *arvit* is evening prayer. The format of the prayers is set out in the **Siddur** and each prayer includes the *Shema* and the *Amidah*, and readings from the Torah and the Nevi'im. The prayers can be said either in the synagogue or at home.

In Orthodox families the prayers are said in Hebrew and males wear their **tefillin** and **tallit** for the *shacharit* prayers. In Liberal/Reform families the prayers are said in English and *tefillin* and *tallit* are optional.

Saying prayers in a set form which has been used for centuries and at set times has many advantages. It:
- stops prayer being focused on selfish concerns
- gives the worshipper a sense of being part of Jewish history
- gives the prayer a sense of community with Jews all over the world
- gives order and purpose to people's religious life.

Saying prayers in your own words whenever you want to is important because people can have a relationship with God only if they can:
- contact God when they want
- express their own thoughts and feelings rather than other people's
- ask for God's help.

Arvit Evening prayer.

Mezuzah Small scroll of the *Shema* fixed to the doorpost of the rooms in a Jewish house.

Minchah Afternoon prayer.

Shacharit Morning prayer.

Siddur The daily prayer book.

Tallit Prayer shawl.

Tefillin Leather boxes containing parts of the Torah strapped on arms and head for prayers.

Sources of wisdom and authority

In Psalm 55 the Psalmist says he prays morning, noon and evening.

Psalm 55 says that people should cast their cares on the Lord and he will sustain them.

Now test yourself

1 A mezuzah is:
   (a) A prayer shawl
   (b) Leather boxes containing parts of the Torah strapped on arms and head for prayers
   (c) Evening prayer
   (d) A small scroll of the *Shema* fixed to the doorpost of the rooms in a Jewish house

2 Arvit is:
   (a) A prayer shawl
   (b) Leather boxes containing parts of the Torah strapped on arms and head for prayers
   (c) Evening prayer
   (d) A small scroll of the *Shema* fixed to the doorpost of the rooms in a Jewish house

3 *Tallit* is:
   (a) A prayer shawl
   (b) Leather boxes containing parts of the Torah strapped on arms and head for prayers
   (c) Evening prayer
   (d) A small scroll of the *Shema* fixed to the doorpost of the rooms in a Jewish house

4 *Tefillin* are:
   (a) A prayer shawl
   (b) Leather boxes containing parts of the Torah strapped on arms and head for prayers
   (c) Evening prayer
   (d) A small scroll of the *Shema* fixed to the doorpost of the rooms in a Jewish house

Activities

Complete the answers to these questions:

1 Outline **three** purposes of prayer for Jewish people.

One purpose of prayer is for Jewish people to build up their relationship with God. Another purpose is for them to serve God with all their heart. A third purpose is

take the opportunities to speak directly to God

2 Explain **two** reasons why it is important for Jewish people to have different forms of prayer. In your answer you must refer to a source of wisdom and authority.

It is important to have different forms because saying prayers in a set form which has been used in this form for centuries and at set times gives order and purpose to people's religious life. As the Psalmist said in Psalm 55, Jews should pray morning, noon and evening. However, saying prayers in your own words whenever you want to is important because

Exam support

You might be asked to evaluate a statement such as: *'God doesn't need people to pray to him.'* This table might help answer such a question:

Arguments for	Arguments against
● God is an infinite being who cannot need the prayers of finite beings. ● God is perfect so he cannot need to be praised by people who are far from perfect. ● God is omniscient so he knows what people need and want without them asking him. ● God is all-good so he does not need prayers to thank him for his goodness, and he will help people without being asked.	● The Mitzvot say that Jews should pray to God at regular times. ● Prayer is a way for people to communicate with God and build a relationship with him. ● Prayer is a way for people to express their thanks and devotion to God. ● Prayer is a way for Jewish people to serve God with their heart, so obeying God's commandment: 'to love the Lord your God and to serve him with all your heart and with all your soul'.

The *Shema* is known as the fundamental prayer of Judaism and emphasises the:

- oneness of God
- need for Jewish people to love God
- covenant God has made with the Jewish people
- need to follow the Mitzvot and teach them to children
- need to pray with *tefillin* and *tallit*
- need for mezuzah.

The Shema is said three times every day (morning prayer, evening prayer and before sleep).

The first two paragraphs are written on the mezuzah scroll and so they are remembered every time a Jew goes into the house and from room to room. The first sentence is said whenever the Torah scroll is taken from the Ark.

The Shema is important because it is a prayer which praises God and expresses faith and trust in God and is also a declaration of the main points of the Jewish faith that there is only one God and that people should love God and follow his commands. This belief that there is only one God who demands moral obedience is often called '**ethical monotheism**' and is the basis of Judaism.

The *Amidah* is the second most important prayer and is sometimes known as 'the **standing** prayer'. It contains 19 blessings which praise God and make personal requests for forgiveness of sins, healing for the sick, food for the world, the coming of the Messiah, peace, goodness, blessings, kindness and compassion.

The prayer should be said standing, facing Jerusalem. The whole prayer is said for weekday daily prayers, with slight amendments on *Shabbat* and festivals. The final section of every *Amidah* concludes with thanksgiving to God requesting him to grant peace, goodness, blessing and compassion for everyone.

The Amidah is important to Jews because it fulfils all the requirements of a prayer set out by the great rabbis (it should begin with words of praise, then ask petitions and end with words of thanks). In addition, people have two needs, the spiritual and the physical – the *Amidah* asks God to fulfil spiritual needs such as forgiveness and physical needs such as food.

Amidah The standing prayer.

Ethical monotheism Belief in one God who demands moral obedience.

Shema The major prayer affirming belief in one God.

Sources of wisdom and authority

The Shema, from Deuteronomy 6 begins: 'Hear, O Israel, the L-rd is our G-d, the L-rd is One. You shall love the L-rd your G-d with all your heart, with all your soul, and with all your might. And these words which I command you today shall be upon your heart.'

Now test yourself

1 The standing prayer is known as:
   (a) Siddur
   (b) *Shema*
   (c) Ethical monotheism
   (d) *Amidah*

2 Belief in one God who demands moral obedience is:
   (a) Siddur
   (b) *Shema*
   (c) Ethical monotheism
   (d) *Amidah*

3 The major prayer affirming belief in one God is the:
   (a) Siddur
   (b) *Shema*
   (c) Ethical monotheism
   (d) *Amidah*

4 The daily prayer book is called the:
   (a) Siddur
   (b) *Shema*
   (c) Ethical monotheism
   (d) *Amidah*

Activities

Complete the answers to these questions:

1 Outline **three** features of the *Amidah*.

The Amidah contains 19 blessings. It should be said standing. It should be said facing

....

2 Explain **two** reasons why the *Shema* is important for Jewish people. In your answer you must refer to a source of wisdom and authority.

The Shema is important because it is a prayer which declares the main points of the Jewish faith that there is only one God. As Deuteronomy chapter 6 says, 'Hear O Israel, the Lord our God, the Lord is One.'

Another reason is

....

....

Exam support

You might be asked to compare and contrast Christian and Jewish worship. Worship in Liberal/Reform synagogues is very similar to Christian worship. This table might help answer such a question on Orthodox Jewish worship:

Differences	Similarities
• Orthodox Jews worship in Hebrew, whereas Christians worship in their native language. • Men and women worship separately in Orthodox Judaism whereas the sexes worship together in Christianity. • The Jewish special day for worship is Saturday whereas the Christian special day is Sunday. • Jews should worship three times a day at set times whereas Christians are required to go to church on Sunday only but are expected to pray every morning and evening. • Christian worship usually has musical accompaniment and often has hymns, while Orthodox Jewish worship does not.	• Worship involves readings from the scriptures in both faiths. • Weekly worship includes a sermon in both faiths. • Worship involves the whole congregation saying a prayer together (even non-liturgical Christian worship includes saying the Lord's Prayer). • Both worships involve praying for the needs of others.

Topic 2.2b.5 Rituals and ceremonies

This topic is all about Jewish rites of passage, rituals which mark the transition from one phase of life to another (births, reaching adulthood, marriage and death). All religions and cultures mark and celebrate these passages in life, both because they are occasions which require marking and because they provide an opportunity for strengthening the society or religion concerned.

Birth ceremonies

Male children are circumcised eight days after their birth in a ceremony known as **Brit Milah** when the **mohel** (circumciser) carries out the operation and then blesses the child and names him. This ceremony marks Jewish males' entry into the covenant. Some very liberal Reform Jews do not circumcise their sons as they believe the covenant with Abraham was purely spiritual.

Female children of Orthodox Jews have a special naming ceremony in the synagogue on the *Shabbat* following the birth. But many Reform/Liberal synagogues have a special **Brit Bat** ceremony for girls to make the occasion as important as Brit Milah.

The Brit Milah and Brit Bat bring a child into the community of Judaism and are important in giving the parents the promise of support from the Jewish community in bringing up this new life in the Jewish faith.

Although any adult male wanting to convert to Judaism must be circumcised, the halakhah makes clear that any male child born Jewish but not circumcised is still a Jew.

Coming of age

Bar Mitzvah is when a boy becomes responsible for his own actions and is regarded as an adult as far as religion is concerned, so he can make up a *minyan*, can read the *sidra* in synagogue services and wear *tallit* and *tefillin*. A boy becomes Bar Mitzvah (son of the commandment) at the age of 13 whether there is a special ceremony or not, but most Jewish families make sure there is a celebration when their son reads the *sidra* from the Torah and the rabbi talks about the joys and responsibilities of being a Jew.

Girls have a **Bat Mitzvah** (daughter of the commandment) ceremony. In Orthodox Judaism girls attain their Bat Mitzvah at the age of 12 but do not assume the same duties as boys. However, in Liberal/Reform Judaism a girl's Bat Mitzvah is just the same as a boy's and happens at the age of 13.

The Bar and Bat Mitzvah are important because they give a young Jewish person the opportunity to take upon themselves the responsibility of being a Jew and ensure the continuity of the Jewish faith.

Bar Mitzvah Son of the commandment, a Jewish boy's coming of age.

Bat Mitzvah Daughter of the commandment, a Jewish girl's coming of age.

Brit Bat A baby girl's entry into the Jewish covenant in Liberal/Reform synagogues.

Brit Milah Covenant of circumcision.

Minyan The required number of adult Jewish males for certain prayers to be said in the synagogue.

Mohel Person trained to perform Brit Milah.

Sources of wisdom and authority

God said to Abraham, 'This is my covenant with you and your descendants after you, the covenant you are to keep. Every male among you shall be circumcised.'

The Midrash says as soon as he becomes of age Jewish fathers bring him into the synagogue and school in order that he may praise the name of God.

Now test yourself

1 Bar Mitzvah is:
   (a) A person trained to perform Brit Milah
   (b) Son of the commandment, a Jewish boy's coming of age
   (c) The covenant of circumcision
   (d) Daughter of the commandment, a Jewish girl's coming of age

2 Bat Mitzvah is:
   (a) A person trained to perform Brit Milah
   (b) Son of the commandment, a Jewish boy's coming of age
   (c) The covenant of circumcision
   (d) Daughter of the commandment, a Jewish girl's coming of age

3 Brit Milah is:
   (a) A person trained to perform Brit Milah
   (b) Son of the commandment, a Jewish boy's coming of age
   (c) The covenant of circumcision
   (d) Daughter of the commandment, a Jewish girl's coming of age

4 A mohel is:
   (a) A person trained to perform Brit Milah
   (b) Son of the commandment, a Jewish boy's coming of age
   (c) The covenant of circumcision
   (d) Daughter of the commandment, a Jewish girl's coming of age

Activities

Complete the answer to this question:

1 Explain **two** reasons why the Brit Milah is important for Jewish people. In your answer you must refer to a source of wisdom and authority.

The Brit Milah is important because it brings baby boys into the community of Judaism. The Torah records that God said to Abraham, 'This is my covenant with you and your descendants after you, the covenant you are to keep. Every male among you shall be circumcised.'

Another reason is that it's important in giving the parents the promise of support from the community of Judaism in bringing up this new life in Jewish faith.

Exam support

You might be asked to evaluate a statement such as: *'Jewish birth ceremonies should be the same for boys and girls.'* This table might help answer such a question:

Arguments for	Arguments against
● Equality of the sexes is now a legal requirement and religion should reflect this. ● Having different ceremonies for boys makes it appear that boys are better than girls. ● Reform/Liberal Jews have a Brit Bat ceremony, so why not the Orthodox as well?	● God made the covenant of circumcision with Abraham. ● There is a mitzvah that male children should be circumcised and Orthodox Jews should follow the Mitzvot. ● The covenant was made by God and it does not mention girls. ● Religious people believe that God's laws supersede human laws.

Marriage ceremonies

There is a mitzvah that all Jews should marry and have children. Marriage is regarded as essential for people to become complete. The ceremony takes place under a canopy called a **huppah**, which symbolises the couple's new home and how marriage needs both privacy and openness to friends and community.

The main feature of the marriage ceremony is the **ketubah**, in which the groom promises to provide for his wife and specifies what she will receive in the event of his death or a divorce. The rabbi recites seven blessings over a glass of wine for such things as making the marriage a happy one which produces children. An Orthodox Jewish wedding ceremony can only take place between two Jews, but some Liberal synagogues have special ceremonies for mixed (inter-faith) marriages.

Jewish marriage ceremonies are important because they bring two people together in the Jewish faith and provide the opportunity for a new Jewish family to develop and continue the faith.

Death and mourning rituals

At the point of death the family say special prayers. As soon as they hear of a death, close relatives make a tear in their clothes to fulfil the mitzvah, then the **chevra kaddisha** helps prepare the body for burial which should take place as soon after death as possible (the Orthodox do not allow cremation). Someone stays with the body all the time until the funeral.

The funeral itself is very simple. The rabbi gives a short speech about the dead person. Then everyone accompanies the body to the grave where prayers are said.

There is a period of mourning (**avelut**) – the first seven days are extreme mourning (**shiva**) when close family sit on low chairs, do not leave the house, mirrors are covered and music is not allowed. For the next three weeks male mourners go to synagogue every day to pray **kaddish**. During this time a simple headstone should be set up in the cemetery.

On the anniversary of the death and as long as mourners live they keep **yarzheit**. On this day the family remembers their dead relative and a candle is kept burning for a night and a day and kaddish is said.

Many Liberal/Reform Jews think that some of the Orthodox funeral customs are out of place in the modern world. So they allow more time to elapse before the funeral so that all family members can attend. They also allow cremation, put on a black ribbon rather than tearing their clothes, sit shiva for only one day and do not use low chairs, do not cover the mirrors, do not stay in the house for seven days and allow music to be played.

Jewish death and funeral rituals are important because the death of a family member is a time of great grief but the rituals of the faith provide the comfort of the Jewish community, which helps people to cope with this terrible time. The rituals also remind them of the Jewish belief that death is not the end and there is still a hope for the future.

Avelut The mourning period.

Chevra kaddisha Burial society.

Huppah Wedding canopy.

Kaddish The prayer recited publicly by mourners.

Ketubah Marriage contract.

Shiva The seven days of intense mourning.

Yarzheit The anniversary day of someone's death.

Sources of wisdom and authority

'For this reason a man will leave his father and mother and be united to his wife and they will become one flesh.' Genesis 2:23–24.

The Talmud says, 'A man without a wife is incomplete. An unmarried woman is an unfinished vessel.'

The Torah records that when Jacob heard that his favourite son, Joseph, was dead, 'Then Jacob tore his clothes, put on sackcloth and mourned for his son many days.' Genesis 37:34.

Now test yourself

1 A huppah is:
   (a) A wedding canopy
   (b) Seven days of intense mourning
   (c) The marriage contract
   (d) A burial society
2 The ketubah is:
   (a) A wedding canopy
   (b) Seven days of intense mourning
   (c) The marriage contract
   (d) A burial society
3 Chevra kaddisha is:
   (a) A wedding canopy
   (b) Seven days of intense mourning
   (c) The marriage contract
   (d) A burial society
4 Shiva is:
   (a) A wedding canopy
   (b) Seven days of intense mourning
   (c) The marriage contract
   (d) A burial society

Activities

Complete the answers to these questions:

1 Outline **three** features of a Jewish wedding ceremony.

One feature is that the marriage ceremony takes place under a canopy called a huppah. A second feature is that the couple must sign the ketubah or marriage contract. A third feature is

....

2 Explain **two** reasons why funeral rituals are important for Jewish people. In your answer you must refer to a source of wisdom and authority.

Jewish death and funeral rituals are important because the death of a family member is a time of great grief but the rituals of the faith provide the comfort of the Jewish community, which helps people to cope with this terrible time as they follow the example of Jacob. The Torah records that when Jacob heard that his favourite son, Joseph, was dead, 'Then Jacob tore his clothes, put on sackcloth and mourned for his son many days.'

Another reason is

....

....

....

Exam support

You might be asked to evaluate a statement such as: *'We don't need religious ceremonies to mark rites of passage nowadays.'* This table might help answer such a question:

Arguments for	Arguments against
● Lots of people mark a birth with a baby shower. ● Legally people come of age at 18 and most people have a big 18th birthday party. ● Most weddings are now non-religious. ● Many people now have non-religious funerals because the person who died had no religious beliefs.	● A religious element makes the event seem more important. ● Religious birth rituals make the relatives more aware that the child has been born into a community as well as a family. ● A religious wedding ceremony brings in God and members of the faith to help the couple make their marriage work. ● A religious funeral gives a hope that death is not the end, even if the people there don't really believe it.

Topic 2.2b.6 *Shabbat*

Shabbat means ceasing from work. Genesis says God created everything in six days and rested on the seventh. The seventh day of the week is Saturday, but for Jews *Shabbat* begins at sunset on Friday and ends at sunset on Saturday.

The Orthodox have 39 categories of work which must be avoided on *Shabbat*, including such things as switching on lights and driving cars. Liberal Jews take a much more relaxed attitude to *Shabbat* observance and will switch on lights and TVs, cook meals and drive to synagogue.

How *Shabbat* is celebrated

- *Shabbat* begins with the woman of the home lighting the *Shabbat* candles and welcoming *Shabbat* into the home.
- On *Shabbat* morning families go to synagogue for the morning prayer, which is the main service of the week. The high point of the service is when the **Sefer Torah** is taken out of the Ark and carried to the bimah for the rabbi to read the **sidra**. A man is called to read from one of the books of the prophets and after the Sefer Torah has been put back in the Ark, the rabbi gives a sermon.
- Liberal synagogues have differences in the services: prayers are said in English, not Hebrew, women sit with the men, the rabbi may well be a woman and some of the prayers may be missed out.
- *Shabbat* worship continues at home with the *Shabbat* meal when the father of the household blesses the children and says **Kiddush** over the wine and blesses **challot** bread. The wine symbolises the sweetness and joy of the day; the *challot* remind the family of the time in the wilderness when God sent two lots of manna on *Shabbat*.
- When night falls the **havdalah** ceremony takes place. The father says a blessing over a cup of wine, then another over the havdalah spice box and a final one over a lighted candle. *Shabbat* begins and ends with wine and lighted candles. The spice box is passed round the family so that the memory of *Shabbat* lingers into the week.

Shabbat **is important for Jewish people because it:**
- is a Mitzvot, the fourth of the Ten Commandments
- gives Jewish people a chance to renew themselves as they rest from work and concentrate on religion
- gives people a chance to think about what they want life to be about
- provides time for a person to think about God and find out more about their faith
- offers an opportunity to socialise outside the demands and pressures of work.

Shabbat **is important for the Jewish community because it:**
- is the oldest Jewish festival, making it important for the community to keep it going
- is God's gift to the Jewish people which binds them together – only Jews celebrate Shabbat
- reminds Jews of when they were slaves in Egypt – refraining from work is a sign of freedom
- offers families the chance to grow together in their Jewish faith.

The fourth commandment says, 'Remember the Sabbath day by keeping it holy. Six days you shall labour and do all your work, but the seventh day is a Sabbath to the LORD your God.'

Challot Plaited loaves used on *Shabbat* and festivals.

Havdalah Ceremony marking the ending of *Shabbat*.

Kiddush A prayer said over wine to sanctify *Shabbat*.

Sefer Torah The Torah scroll kept in the Ark.

Sidra A passage from the Torah.

Sources of wisdom and authority

The fourth commandment says, 'Remember the Sabbath day by keeping it holy. Six days you shall labour and do all your work, but the seventh day is a Sabbath to the LORD your God.'

Now test yourself

1 Plaited loaves used on *Shabbat* and festivals are called|:
   (a) Havdalah
   (b) *Sidra*
   (c) *Challot*
   (d) Kiddush

2 The ceremony marking the ending of *Shabbat* is:
   (a) Havdalah
   (b) *Sidra*
   (c) *Challot*
   (d) Kiddush

3 A prayer said over wine to sanctify *Shabbat* is called:
   (a) Havdalah
   (b) *Sidra*
   (c) *Challot*
   (d) Kiddush

4 A passage from the Torah is called:
   (a) Havdalah
   (b) *Sidra*
   (c) *Challot*
   (d) Kiddush

Activities

Complete the answers to these questions:

1 Outline **three** things Orthodox Jews cannot do on *Shabbat*.

Orthodox Jews cannot go to work on Shabbat. They also cannot switch on electricity. A third thing is

....

2 Explain **two** reasons why *Shabbat* is important for Jews. In your answer you must refer to a source of wisdom and authority.

Shabbat is important for Jewish people because resting on Shabbat is a mitzvah which all Orthodox Jews must keep. The fourth commandment says, 'Remember the Sabbath day by keeping it holy. Six days you shall labour and do all your work, but the seventh day is a Sabbath to the Lord your God.'

Another reason is

....

....

....

Exam support

You might be asked to evaluate a statement such as: 'Shabbat *should be about worshipping God, not keeping rules.*' This table might help answer such a question:

Arguments for	Arguments against
• The first mitzvah is to love God with all your heart and soul, not to keep rules. • People's relationship with God is more important than not driving a car to *Shabbat* service. • It is impossible for some people (emergency services, electricity suppliers, etc.) not to work on *Shabbat*. • The modern world requires seven-day working, but that does not stop people from worshipping God. Loving God and loving your neighbour have to be more important.	• Keeping rules is the basis of Orthodox Judaism. • God gave Moses the 613 Mitzvot for Jewish people to obey as their part of the Mosaic Covenant so people have to keep the rules. • If God gave the rules, then people cannot cherry pick which ones to obey. If you are part of the Jewish community, you have to obey the rules. • For Orthodox Jews, keeping the rules is part of worshipping God, the two cannot be separated.

Topic 2.2b.7 Festivals

Rosh Hashanah marks the beginning of Jewish New Year and has been celebrated since biblical times. It remembers when Moses went up Mount Sinai to receive new tablets of the Ten Commandments to replace the ones after the Israelites worshipped the golden calf. Forty days later (**Yom Kippur**) he returned with the new tablets, showing that God had forgiven the people because they had repented.

In the month before Rosh Hashanah the **shofar** is blown every day in the synagogue and people think about their sins and their relationships with God and people. They make new year resolutions and throw their sins into the water in the **tashlich** ceremony.

Rosh Hashanah is important because it is a chance for a person to come before God, acknowledge what they have done wrong and show how they are going to do good in the coming year.

Yom Kippur occurs ten days after Rosh Hashanah. These are known as 'the **days of awe**', when people reflect on what they promised at Rosh Hashanah.

Yom Kippur is commanded in the Torah and in the days of the Temple the priests sacrificed a bull as a sin offering and sent a scapegoat into the wilderness, symbolically taking the people's sins. Nowadays Yom Kippur involves:

- a 25-hour fast
- reflection of past sins
- confession of sins and prayers for forgiveness
- no jewellery or leather shoes (forbidden in Leviticus)
- a special evening service in the synagogue, including the **Kol Nidrei** prayer.

Yom Kippur is important because:

- the mizvot say that those who do not fast on Yom Kippur must be cut off from the people
- it releases people from guilt about the sins of the past
- fasting encourages the self-discipline needed to keep the resolutions made at Rosh Hashanah
- fasting helps people to feel compassion for the poor.

After the Israelites escaped from Egypt at the Exodus, they spent 40 years as nomads in the wilderness, living in temporary huts (**sukkot**) roofed with palm leaves. The Sukkot festival takes Jewish people back to those times as families live in their sukkah.

The festival, which begins five days after Yom Kippur, is commanded in the Torah. On each day of the festival people meet in the synagogue carrying an **etrog** in one hand and a **lulav** as commanded in the mitzvah. They wave the lulav in all directions and there is much rejoicing (sukkot is called 'the season of our rejoicing').

Sukkot is important because:

- it encourages family harmony by living in a sukkah
- it is a link with the ancestors
- the etrog stands for people who both know the Torah and do good deeds, the lulav stands for those who are learned in Torah but do no good deeds
- the four species (lulav, myrtle, willow and etrog) symbolise God's presence everywhere and the blessings he showers on his people.

Days of awe The ten days between Rosh Hashanah and Yom Kippur.

Etrog A citron fruit.

Kol Nidrei Annulment of vows made before Yom Kippur.

Lulav Palm branch.

Shofar Ram's horn.

Sukkot Singular sukkah, a temporary dwelling, also known as a tabernacle.

Tashlich Casting away sins into running water.

Yom Kippur The Day of Atonement.

Sources of wisdom and authority

'It is the Day of Atonement, when atonement is made for you before the Lord your God. Anyone who does not deny himself on that day must be cut off from his people.' Leviticus 23:26–29.

Leviticus orders a seven-day festival for Sukkot when people must live in Sukkot for the whole seven days and celebrate with lulav.

Now test yourself

1 Etrog is:
   (a) A citron fruit
   (b) Annulment of vows made before Yom Kippur
   (c) A ram's horn
   (d) Casting away sins into running water
2 Shofar is:
   (a) A citron fruit
   (b) Annulment of vows made before Yom Kippur
   (c) A ram's horn
   (d) Casting away sins into running water

3 Tashlich is:
   (a) A citron fruit
   (b) Annulment of vows made before Yom Kippur
   (c) A ram's horn
   (d) Casting away sins into running water
4 Kol Nidrei is:
   (a) A citron fruit
   (b) Annulment of vows made before Yom Kippur
   (c) A ram's horn
   (d) Casting away sins into running water

Activities

Complete the answers to these questions:
1 Outline **three** features of the festival of Sukkot.

One feature of Sukkot is that families build a temporary home. A second feature is that they live in the temporary home for the seven days of the festival. A third feature is

....

2 Explain **two** reasons why Yom Kippur is important for Jewish people. In your answer you must refer to a source of wisdom and authority.

Yom Kippur is important for Jewish people because it is a festival for which there are Mitzvot. Indeed, it is one which all Jews should observe because as the Torah says in Leviticus, those who do not fast on Yom Kippur must be cut off from the people.

Another reason is

....

....

....

Exam support

You might be asked to evaluate a statement such as: *'You can't be considered a Jew if you don't fast and go to synagogue on Yom Kippur.'* This table might help answer such a question:

Arguments for	Arguments against
• Leviticus says that anyone who does not fast on Yom Kippur must be cut off from the people, that is no longer be considered a Jew. • There are lots of Mitzvot about Yom Kippur so all Jews should observe it. • All the Jewish community observes Yom Kippur so if you don't, you are putting yourself outside the community.	• Some Jews do not have a synagogue to go to because they live in a non-Jewish area. • Anyone who is ill is not allowed to fast. • The principle of *pikuach nefesh* means people in emergency services cannot fast for 25 hours if they are on duty. • Liberal/Reform Jews might think these Mitzvot can be ignored as they don't believe they come from God, but they are still Jews.

Pesach is a seven-day festival at the beginning of spring. In the days before Pesach houses are cleaned to remove all traces of leaven (**chametz**) and children have special games hunting for any chametz in the house.

Pesach is an important festival remembering Israel's enslavement in Egypt, Moses and the Exodus when God saved Israel and gave the people their freedom (Pesach is sometimes called the freedom festival).

What happens:
- Pesach is welcomed into the home just like *Shabbat*.
- A synagogue service is held during which there are special prayers to thank God for freeing their ancestors from slavery in Egypt.
- The family return for the great meal of Pesach (the **seder**), which follows an order as set out in the **Hagadah** book and has special foods on the seder plate. The youngest family member asks a series of questions and the father answers them. The family sing songs about the Exodus and at the end of the roast lamb meal they eat the **afikomen**.
- Unleavened bread is eaten for seven days, then there is a havdalah ceremony, after which those families who have been using special Pesach crockery wash it and put it away.
- In the Seder meal, charoset (fruit and nut paste) represents the mud bricks the Israelite slaves had to make, bitter herbs represent the pain of slavery, burnt egg represents the temple sacrifices, lamb shank represents the lambs sacrificed at Passover, green parsley and lettuce represent freedom.

Pesach is important because it celebrates:
- God's power and control of history – without the Passover and Exodus there would be no Jewish people
- the birthday of the Jewish nation
- with the seder meal like a birthday party for the nation
- Jewish history and the way God has preserved his chosen people.

Shavuot is the Feast of Weeks, celebrated seven weeks after Passover. It began as a harvest festival, but seven weeks after the events of the Exodus celebrated at Pesach, Moses was given the Torah on Mount Sinai and this is now the main element of the festival – thanking God for the gift of the Torah.

Shavuot is the only festival without a specific mitzvah ordering its celebration because the giving of the Torah is so important that celebrating the giving of it is required by all 613 Mitzvot.

The main things that happen at Shavuot are:
- candles are lit to bring in the festival
- many people stay up to read the Torah on the first night
- everyone goes to synagogue on the first day to hear the reading of the Ten Commandments
- people eat dairy foods rather than meat.
- on the second day prayers are said for those who have died
- the Book of Ruth is read.

Shavuot is important because:
- the gift of the Torah is the most important thing in Jewish history
- while Pesach gave the Israelites physical freedom, Shavuot celebrates the spiritual freedom brought by the Mitzvot.

Afikomen A piece of unleavened bread eaten at the end of the seder meal.

Chametz Any food containing yeast/leaven.

Hagadah Book telling the story of the first Passover.

Pesach Passover.

Seder The Passover meal.

Sources of wisdom and authority

Leviticus says that the Lord's Passover lasts for seven days and that for that time 'you must eat bread made without yeast'.

Exodus says that for the seven days of Passover 'no yeast is to be found in your house. And whoever eats anything made with yeast in it must be cut off from the community of Israel'.

Deuteronomy says that Jewish people should 'sacrifice as the Passover to the Lord your God an animal from their flock or herd'.

Now test yourself

1 The piece of unleavened bread eaten at the end of the seder meal is called:
   (a) Pesach
   (b) Hagadah
   (c) Afikomen
   (d) Chametz

2 Any food containing yeast/leaven is known as:
   (a) Pesach
   (b) Hagadah
   (c) Afikomen
   (d) Chametz

3 The book telling the story of the first Passover is:
   (a) Pesach
   (b) Hagadah
   (c) Afikomen
   (d) Chametz

4 The Passover festival is known as what in Hebrew?
   (a) Pesach
   (b) Hagadah
   (c) Afikomen
   (d) Chametz

Activities

Complete the answers to these questions:

1 Outline **three** features of the Seder meal.

One feature is that there are special foods on the seder plate. A second feature is that the youngest family member asks a series of questions which are answered by the father.

A third feature is

the family sing songs about the Exodus.

2 Explain **two** reasons why Shavuot is important for Jewish people. In your answer you must refer to a source of wisdom and authority.

Shavuot is important because it celebrates the gift of the Torah to the Jewish people. The 613 Mitzvot contained in the five books of Moses which make up the Torah are the most important thing in Jewish history and are the basis of the Jewish faith.

Another reason is

while pesach gave the Israelites physical freedom, Shavuot celebrates the spiritual freedom brought by the mitzvot.

Exam support

You might be asked to evaluate a statement such as: *'Pesach is the most important Jewish festival.'* This table might help answer such a question:

Arguments for	Arguments against
Pesach is the most important festival because: • it celebrates the Passover and Exodus, without which there would be no Judaism or Jewish people • it demonstrates God's power and control of history • it celebrates the Exodus, which is the birthday of the Jewish nation, and the seder meal is like a birthday party for the nation • it celebrates Jewish history and the way God has preserved his chosen people.	It could be argued that: • Rosh Hashanah is more important because it is a chance to acknowledge what you have done wrong and show how you are going to do good in the coming year • Yom Kippur is more important because the Torah says in Leviticus those who do not fast on Yom Kippur must be cut off from the people • Shavuot is more important because it celebrates the gift of the Torah, which is the most important thing in Jewish history.

Topic 2.2b.8 Features of the synagogue

Exterior synagogue design

Any synagogue should have a Star of David or a **menorah** to show it is Jewish, be built facing Jerusalem where the Temple stood and have windows letting in the light so that worship is not a retreat from the world.

Interior synagogue design

All synagogues should have these features:

- a sink at the entrance for worshippers to ceremonially cleanse themselves
- the Holy Ark (**Aron Hakodesh**) as the focal centre of the synagogue, often with an embroidered black and gold curtain in front – inside the Ark are the Torah scrolls (Sefer Torah)
- a **yad** so the holy words of the Sefer Torah will not be touched by dirty fingers
- a **bimah** with a desk for reading the Torah, a chair on one side for the rabbi and on the other side for the **chazzan or cantor** who leads the prayers – the bimah is usually in front of the Ark
- above the Ark, the **ner tamid** representing the menorah in the Jerusalem Temple whose seven wicks were never allowed to go out
- an actual menorah on a lampstand with six or eight branches instead of the Temple menorah's seven, because the Orthodox think exact copies of the Temple objects are wrong
- on the wall next to or above the Ark, usually the words of the Ten Commandments.

Aron Hakodesh The Ark.

Bimah The raised platform for Torah readings.

Chazan/cantor The leader of worship who chants the prayers.

Menorah Seven-branched candlestick.

Ner tamid The everlasting light.

Yad Pointer for reading the Sefer Torah.

Sources of wisdom and authority

The Torah says in Exodus 27 that the lamps in the sanctuary must be kept burning from morning to evening.

Exodus 27 says there must be a curtain shielding the Ark.

How the synagogue is used by the different communities

Orthodox	Liberal/Reform
Separate seating for women, sometimes with a screen between the men's and women's sections.	Men and women sit together.
The rabbi and cantor will always be men.	The rabbi and/or cantor may be women.
No musical instruments played on *Shabbat* because that would be work.	There may be an organ or a piano or a band for *Shabbat* worship.
Only males will be asked up to read.	Both men and women can be asked up to read.
Synagogues prayers will be in Hebrew.	Prayers will be mainly in English.
Prayers for the rebuilding of the Temple and the return of all Jewish people to the Holy Land.	Such prayers are no longer said.
Only men carry the Torah scrolls.	Women or girls may be invited to carry the Torah scrolls.
People will have walked to synagogue.	Many will have come by car.

How else the synagogue is used

Most synagogues have classrooms for learning Hebrew, for lessons preparing for Bat/Bar Mitzvah, and for meetings and lectures to learn more about the faith. Many synagogues have a hall for wedding and Bar/Bat Mitzvah celebrations. It is also used for mother and toddler groups, senior citizens' clubs and other community activities.

Now test yourself

1 The Ark containing the Sefer Torah is called the:
   (a) Ner tamid
   (b) Yad
   (c) Bimah
   (d) Aron Hakodesh

2 The raised platform for Torah readings is called the:
   (a) Ner tamid
   (b) Yad
   (c) Bimah
   (d) Aron Hakodesh

3 The everlasting light above the Ark is called:
   (a) Ner tamid
   (b) Yad
   (c) Bimah
   (d) Aron Hakodesh

4 The pointer for reading the Sefer Torah is called the:
   (a) Ner tamid
   (b) Yad
   (c) Bimah
   (d) Aron Hakodesh

Activities

Complete the answers to these questions:

1 Outline **three** objects of devotion used within the synagogue.

One object is the Ark Hakodesh, containing the Sefer Torah. Another object is the everlasting light of the Ner Tamid. A third feature is

Yad so the holy words of the Sefer Torah will not be touched by dirty fingers

2 Explain **two** reasons why the synagogue is used differently by different communities. In your answer you must refer to a source of wisdom and authority.

The Orthodox and Liberal Reform use the synagogue differently. For example, the Orthodox do not allow music on *Shabbat* because they consider playing an instrument to be work, which is banned by the fourth of the Ten Commandments in Exodus chapter 20.

Another reason is that

Orthodox seperate seating for women, sometimes with a screen between the men's and women's seating as for Liberal / Reform Jews in the synagogue Men and women sit together.

Exam support

You might be asked to evaluate a statement such as: *'The synagogue is the most important place for Jewish people.'* This table might help answer such a question:

Arguments for	Arguments against
● Orthodox men go to synagogue three times a day for the daily prayers. ● The highlight of the week is the *Shabbat* service on Saturday when the Jewish community meets together and the Sefer Torah is brought out of the Ark. ● The great festivals of Yom Kippur, Rosh Hashanah and Shavuot require the synagogue to be celebrated properly. ● The synagogue is the place where children are taught Hebrew and the basics of the faith. ● The synagogue is the place where Bar and Bat Mitzvahs, weddings and funerals take place.	● There can't be a synagogue without a *minyan* so for any Jew living in an area with fewer than ten adult male Jews there can't even be a synagogue. ● All the daily prayers can take place in the home. ● Brit Milah and Brit Bat can take place in the home. ● Pesach is celebrated in the home and the other festivals can be celebrated in the home. ● Weddings and funerals only need a rabbi, not a synagogue.

3.1 Arguments for the existence of God

Topic 3.1.1 Revelation as proof of the existence of God

REVISED

The word 'revelation' is used in religion to describe God making himself known to humanity.

Catholics believe that God has revealed himself through:

- **Natural revelation** – the idea that you can look at the world and see signs of God. Religious believers see life as spiritual as well as material. They believe that the vastness of the universe and the beauty of nature are enough to make people believe in God.
- **Special revelation** – the idea that God has revealed himself in special ways, such as sending his word in the Bible.

Christians believe the Bible proves the existence of God because:

- it is inspired by the Holy Spirit, which means it comes from God and reveals God
- the Church teaches that God speaks through both the Old Testament and the New Testament, showing his character and commands
- it contains God's laws on how to behave, such as the Ten Commandments; these rules are there to help people live as God intends so it has authority by showing them how God wants them to live
- it can bring people into a closer relationship with God by learning about what God wants and how God cares for them.

Catholics believe that God's revelation culminated in the Incarnation because:

- all the small revelations found in the Old Testament are summed up and made even clearer in the life of Jesus
- in the Incarnation, God made a complete revelation of himself because the Son is the exact representation of God's being so nothing more can be revealed.

The Church teaches that this means there can be no further revelation of God after Jesus as God's message to humanity reached its highest point in him. So, although there might have been religions formed after the time of Jesus, such as Islam and Sikhism, Catholics cannot agree with all that they teach because even if there is much in these religions that they can respect, God's final truth came in Jesus.

God's revelation in Jesus Christ shows Catholics that God is:

- one whose main characteristic is love as he loved the world so much he became flesh in Jesus Christ
- one who forgives – he was prepared to die on the cross to bring forgiveness for the world's sins
- one who meets people where they are as seen in the way he made disciples of all types and classes of people
- one who brings healing, whether of body, mind or spirit, as seen in the many miracles he performed while on Earth
- one who wants people to have eternal life, which he showed by rising from the dead.

Culminated Reached a point of highest development.

Incarnation The belief that God became man in Christ.

Natural revelation The revealing of God in the nature of the universe.

Special revelation The revealing of God in such things as holy books, for example the Bible.

Sources of wisdom and authority

The Catechism says that it pleased God, in his goodness and wisdom, to reveal himself through Christ, the Word made flesh.

The letter to the Hebrews chapter 1 says that God spoke in the past through the prophets, but has now spoken finally through his Son, who is the exact representation of God.

The Catechism teaches that although God's special revelation is complete after the ascension, there is much about God's nature that Christians will not fully understand until they are in heaven.

Now test yourself

1 To reach a point of highest development is to reach:
   (a) Culmination
   (b) Natural revelation
   (c) Special revelation
   (d) Incarnation

2 The belief that God became man in Christ is known as:
   (a) Culmination
   (b) Natural revelation
   (c) Special revelation
   (d) Incarnation

3 The revealing of God in the nature of the universe is called:
   (a) Culmination
   (b) Natural revelation
   (c) Special revelation
   (d) Incarnation

4 The revealing of God in such things as holy books, for example the Bible, is called:
   (a) Culmination
   (b) Natural revelation
   (c) Special revelation
   (d) Incarnation

Activities

Complete the answers to these questions:

1 Outline **three** characteristics of God shown by the revelation in Jesus Christ.

One characteristic of God shown by the revelation of Jesus is that God is love. Another characteristic is that God is one who brings healing. A third characteristic is

....

2 Explain **two** reasons why Christians believe Jesus is the culmination of God's revelation. In your answer you must refer to a source of wisdom and authority.

One reason is because all the revelations found in the Old Testament are summed up and made even clearer in the life of Jesus. As the Letter to the Hebrews says, God spoke in the past through the prophets, God has now spoken finally through his Son.

Another reason is

....
....

Exam support

You might be asked to evaluate a statement such as: *'The Bible proves that God exists.'* This table might help answer such a question:

Arguments for	Arguments against
• The Church teaches that the Bible is the Word of God and if it is God's Word, God must exist. • The Church teaches that God speaks through both the Old Testament and the New Testament, showing his character and commands. • The Bible can bring people into a closer relationship with God by teaching them about what God wants and how God cares for them, so proving that God exists.	• The Bible can prove God's existence only if it is the Word of God, but there is no evidence for the Church's claim that the Bible is the Word of God except that the Church says it is. • If the Bible was the Word of God, all Bibles would be the same, but Catholics and Protestants disagree about which books should be in the Bible. • The Bible assumes that God exists but it does not give reasons for God existing other than the world being so wonderful it must have been created by God, but that is an opinion, not a proof.

A vision is something seen in a dream, trance or religious ecstasy. Catholics believe that visions are important because God uses visions to give Christians his messages.

There are many visions in the Bible, but the ones you need to know are:

- **Abraham's vision:** Abraham was childless and worried about having no descendants when God appeared to him, took him outside and pointed to the stars in the sky. God then gave him a message of hope, assuring Abraham that he would have a son and would have as many descendants as there were stars in the sky.
- **The Transfiguration:** Jesus took his disciples Peter, James and John up a high mountain where he was transfigured – his face shone like the Sun, and his clothes became as white as the light. The disciples then had a vision of Moses and **Elijah**, talking with Jesus. A bright cloud covered them and a voice from the cloud told them that Jesus was his son and that they must listen to Jesus.

There have been many reported visions since biblical times, including **St Joan of Arc** who was a French peasant girl during the Hundred Years War between England and France. She claimed to have had a vision in which the Archangel Michael, St Margaret and St Catherine told her to drive the English out of France. She managed to convince the French royal court of their truth. She inspired the French armies with her words and led them to several victories before being caught by the English, tried as a **heretic** and burned at the stake. Catholics believe her visions were genuine because the **Vatican** has investigated them three times and declared them to be so. They also feel that it must have been almost impossible for an illiterate peasant girl to do what she did without God's help.

Visions might lead some people to believe in God because:

- they claim to come from God, so if they happen, God must exist
- the changes in the behaviour of the person having the vision (for example St Joan of Arc) make it seem the vision must have come from God
- the message in the vision makes them think it must have come from God
- if the person having the vision is known to be honest, then the vision could only come from God.

Non-religious people such as Atheists and Humanists believe visions do not prove God's existence because:

- people who have mental illness, stress or are on certain types of medication experience **hallucinations** very similar to the visions of saints
- visionaries see the Virgin Mary as blonde and blue eyed but most Middle Eastern Jews had dark eyes, skin and hair
- visions exist only in the mind of the person experiencing them and so prove nothing
- there is no independent evidence for visions.

Catholics disagree with these arguments since the Church's investigations of visions rule out mental illness and drugs and show the visionaries as good people whose visions have a positive effect on others.

Elijah An Old Testament prophet.

Hallucination An experience involving seeing something not really present.

Heretic A person believing something which goes against the accepted beliefs of a religion.

Vatican The headquarters of the Catholic Church.

Sources of wisdom and authority

Abraham's vision comes from Genesis chapter 15.

The Transfiguration comes from St Matthew's Gospel chapter 17.

Now test yourself

1 The Vatican is:
   (a) A person believing something which goes against the accepted beliefs of a religion
   (b) An Old Testament prophet
   (c) The headquarters of the Catholic Church
   (d) An experience involving seeing something not really present

2 A heretic is:
   (a) A person believing something which goes against the accepted beliefs of a religion
   (b) An Old Testament prophet
   (c) The headquarters of the Catholic Church
   (d) An experience involving seeing something not really present

3 A hallucination is:
   (a) A person believing something which goes against the accepted beliefs of a religion
   (b) An Old Testament prophet
   (c) The headquarters of the Catholic Church
   (d) An experience involving seeing something not really present

4 Elijah was:
   (a) A person believing something which goes against the accepted beliefs of a religion
   (b) An Old Testament prophet
   (c) The headquarters of the Catholic Church
   (d) An experience involving seeing something not really present

Activities

Complete the answers to these questions:

1 Outline **three** visions that are important to Catholics.

One important vision was when God told Abraham he would have a son. Another was when St Joan of Arc had a vision of the Archangel Michael telling her to drive the English out of France. A third vision was *of Jesus took his disciples Peter, James and John up the high mountain where he was transfigured. The The third vision this was of disciples having a vision of Moses and Elijah, talking with Jesus.*

2 Explain **two** reasons why Catholics believe visions are important. In your answer you must refer to a source of wisdom and authority.

Catholics believe visions are important because they are one of God's ways of communicating with humans. For example, St Matthew's Gospel records the Transfiguration when the disciples then had a vision of Moses and Elijah talking with Jesus and a voice from the cloud told them that Jesus was his son and that they must listen to Jesus.

Another reason is *that a vision shows God's love for us, were special people — for example Genesis chapter 15 Abraham is told that he'll have a son. A vision proves that God must exist if it's come from God, message also indicates this.*

Exam support

You might be asked to evaluate a statement such as: *'Visions prove that God exists.'* This table might help answer such a question:

Arguments for	Arguments against
• Visions claim to come from God, so if they happen, God must exist.	• People who have mental illness, stress or are on certain types of medication experience hallucinations very similar to the visions of saints.
• The changes to the behaviour of the person having the vision (for example St Joan of Arc) make it seem the vision must have come from God.	• Visionaries see the Virgin Mary as blonde and blue eyed but most Middle Eastern Jews had dark eyes, skin and hair.
• The message in the vision makes them think it must have come from God.	• Visions exist only in the mind of the person experiencing them and so prove nothing.
• If the person having the vision is known to be honest, then the vision could only come from God.	• There is no independent evidence for visions.

Topic 3.1.3 Miracles as proof of the existence of God

A miracle is an event which seems to break a law of science and the only explanation for which seems to be God.

Miracles are a major part of Catholic belief. The Bible shows miracles are bringing about faith and helping faith to grow. The Church's process of **canonisation** depends on being able to establish two miracles connected with the proposed saint.

The Bible is full of miracles, such as the Feeding of the Five Thousand and the Raising of **Lazarus**. In St John's Gospel there is an account of Jesus healing a royal official's son. The son is close to death, so the official asks Jesus to come and save his son. Jesus tells him his son will live; the official goes home and discovers his son recovered, which leads him and his household to believe.

Catholics believe that God still performs miracles. One of the most famous Catholic miracles is that of St Bernadette of Lourdes, who saw an **apparition** of a young woman clothed in brilliant white with a blue girdle. This was followed by 18 apparitions. In one, a miraculous spring arose in a grotto; in another, the woman said she was the **immaculate conception**. Since these miraculous appearances of the Virgin Mary, Lourdes has become a place of pilgrimage for Catholics and many healing miracles are claimed to have taken place there.

Catholics believe that miracles prove God exists because:
- if a miracle has happened, God must have performed the miracle and to perform it he must exist
- only God can perform miracles, so if they happen, God must exist – the miracles authenticated by the Church have been examined scientifically and proven to be true
- if someone witnesses a miracle and they cannot find a natural explanation, they will be forced to believe it was caused by God.

Non-religious people such as Atheists and Humanists argue that:
- miracles are supposed to break the laws of nature, which are based on our whole experience of life, so to believe in a miracle, the evidence for it would have to be stronger than our whole experience of life, but it never is
- the evidence for miracles is always based on the evidence of witnesses, but we know that witnesses can be mistaken or even tell lies
- many miracles from the past can now be explained
- if God really performed miracles, he would surely use them to help remove hunger and poverty rather than just helping the odd sick person.

Catholics disagree with these arguments because they believe:
- they can rely on the truth of biblical miracles because the Bible comes from God
- miracles have been authenticated by the Church
- if God used miracles to stop hunger and war, he would be changing the nature of life.

Apparition A supernatural appearance of a person or thing.

Canonisation The Church's process of declaring someone a new saint.

Immaculate conception The Catholic belief that God preserved Mary from original sin from the moment she was conceived.

Lazarus A friend of Jesus, the brother of Mary and Martha.

Sources of wisdom and authority

The book of Exodus chapter 13 records the parting of the Red Sea.

St John's Gospel records the healing of a royal official's son by Jesus.

The Gospels of Mark and Matthew have an account of Jesus feeding 5000 people with five loaves and two fish.

The Catholic Church has investigated and ratified a large number of miracles in the process of canonising saints.

Now test yourself

1 A supernatural appearance of a person or thing is:
   (a) Canonisation
   (b) Dream
   (c) Apparition
   (d) Deification

2 The Church's process of declaring someone a new saint is:
   (a) Canonisation
   (b) Dream
   (c) Apparition
   (d) Deification

3 The Catholic belief that God preserved Mary from original sin from the moment she was conceived is known as:
   (a) The assumption
   (b) The coronation of the Blessed Virgin
   (c) The immaculate conception
   (d) The virgin birth

4 A friend of Jesus who was the brother of Mary and Martha was:
   (a) Paul
   (b) Barabbas
   (c) Levi
   (d) Lazarus

Activities

Complete the answers to these questions:

1 Outline **three** biblical miracles.

One miracle is Jesus healing a royal official's son. Another biblical miracle is the raising of Lazarus. A third biblical miracle is the feeding of the five thousand.

2 Explain **two** beliefs about God's nature which Catholics believe are shown by miracles. In your answer you must refer to a source of wisdom and authority.

Catholics believe that miracles show God's love for people. For example, John's Gospel records that Jesus raised Lazarus from the dead out of love for Lazarus and his family.

Another belief shown by miracles is that if the miracle has happened, God must have performed the miracle and to perform it, he must exist e.g Jesus healing a royal official's sons.

Exam support

You might be asked to evaluate a statement such as: *'Miracles prove that God exists.'* This table might help answer such a question:

Arguments for	Arguments against
• If a miracle has happened, God must have performed the miracle and to perform it he must exist.	• Miracles are supposed to break the laws of nature, which are based on our whole experience of life, so to believe in a miracle, the evidence for it would have to be stronger than our whole experience of life, but it never is.
• Only God can perform miracles, so if they happen, God must exist.	• The evidence for miracles is always based on the evidence of witnesses, but we know that witnesses can be mistaken or even tell lies.
• If people witness a miracle and they cannot find a natural explanation they will be forced to believe it was caused by God.	• Many miracles from the past can now be explained.
• The miracles authenticated by the Church have been examined scientifically and proven to be true, and if they are true, God must exist.	• If God really performed miracles, he would surely use them to help remove hunger and poverty rather than just helping the odd sick person.

Topic 3.1.4 Catholic attitudes to religious experience

Religious experience is an event that people feel gives them direct contact with God. The clearest types of religious experience are visions and miracles. Other types are:

Conversion is used to describe an experience of God which is so great that the person wants to change his or her life or religion and commit themselves to God in a special way. Conversion experiences make people believe in God because they feel that God is calling them to do something for him.

The **numinous** is a feeling of the presence of God. When people are in a religious building, in a beautiful place or looking up at the stars on a clear night, they may be filled with the awareness that there is something greater than them, which they feel to be God. It is often described as an experience of the **transcendent**. Such a feeling is likely to lead them to believe in God.

Prayer is a religious experience when the person praying feels that God is listening to the prayer. Also an answered prayer (for example, when someone prays for a sick loved one to recover and they do) will lead to belief in God.

Conversion An experience which changes your life or religion.

Numinous The feeling of the presence of something greater than you.

Prayer An attempt to contact God, usually through words.

Transcendent Something going beyond human experience and existing outside the material world.

Most religious people believe religious experience is a proof for God's existence because:
- for people to have a numinous experience, something must be causing the experience and the only possible cause is God
- if a miracle happens, then all the laws of science have been broken and the only explanation for such an event is God, so God must exist
- if a person has such a vivid religious experience that it converts them and totally changes their life, it must have been caused by God
- if a person prays and their prayer is answered, then God must have answered the prayer and so God must exist.

Non-religious people such as Atheists and Humanists do not believe in God and so they do not believe that religious experiences prove God's existence because:
- if numinous experiences came from God, everyone in the same place and the same time would have to have the same experience, but they don't
- they believe that all miracles can be explained, for example Jesus may not have been dead when he was taken down from the cross
- conversion experiences are only in that person's head and cannot prove anything to anyone else
- there are more unanswered prayers than answered ones, so the unanswered prayers prove God does not exist
- followers of all religions claim to have religious experiences so they cannot prove the truth of any one religion.

Catholics disagree with these ideas because they believe everyone has a spiritual sense, they just interpret their experiences differently from religious people. They claim that these experiences prove God exists but cannot prove the truth of any particular religion.

Sources of wisdom and authority

The Catechism claims that religious experiences happen because people are created by God and for God, and God is always trying to contact humans.

The Catechism teaches that religious experiences can be genuine only if they conform with Church doctrines and do not claim to supersede the revelation of Christ.

Now test yourself

1 An experience which changes your life or religion is called:
  (a) Prayer
  (b) Transcendent
  (c) Conversion
  (d) Numinous

2 The feeling of the presence of something greater than you is called:
  (a) Prayer
  (b) Transcendent
  (c) Conversion
  (d) Numinous

3 An attempt to contact God, usually through words, is called:
  (a) Prayer
  (b) Transcendent
  (c) Conversion
  (d) Numinous

4 Something going beyond human experience and existing outside the material world is called:
  (a) Prayer
  (b) Transcendent
  (c) Conversion
  (d) Numinous

Activities

Complete the answer to this question:

1 Explain **two** reasons why not all religious experiences are approved by the Church. In your answer you must refer to a source of wisdom and authority.

A religious experience which contradicted Christian belief (for example, someone having a vision in which God told them not to go to Mass) would not be approved by the Church because it could not possibly come from God.

Another reason is

....

....

....

Exam support

You might be asked to evaluate a statement such as: *'Religious experiences prove that God exists.'* This table might help answer such a question:

Arguments for	Arguments against
● For people to have a numinous experience, something must be causing the experience and the only possible cause is God. ● If a miracle happens, then all the laws of science have been broken and the only explanation for such an event is God, so God must exist. ● If people have such a vivid religious experience that it converts them and totally changes their life, it must have been caused by God. ● If people pray and their prayer is answered, then God must have answered the prayer and so God must exist.	● If numinous experiences came from God, everyone in the same place and the same time would have to have the same experience, but they don't. ● People believe that all miracles can be explained, for example Jesus may not have been dead when he was taken down from the cross. ● Conversion experiences are only in that person's head and cannot prove anything to anyone else. ● There are more unanswered prayers than answered ones, so the unanswered prayers prove God does not exist.

Topic 3.1.5 The design argument

The **design** argument claims that if something seems to be designed, it must have a designer. The universe appears to be designed so it must have a designer, and God is the only possible designer of a universe.

The classic design argument was put forward by William Paley who argued that:
- if you were walking in an uninhabited place and came across a watch, you could not say it had been put there by chance
- the complexity of the watch's mechanism would make you say it must have had a designer
- the universe is a far more complex mechanism than a watch
- so if a watch needs a designer, the universe must definitely need a designer
- the only being that could design the universe would be God
- therefore God must exist.

Some scientists also see evidence of design in the process of **evolution** where complex life forms develop from simple ones. From this they have developed **the modern argument from design**:
- Anything that has been designed needs a designer.
- There is plenty of evidence that the world has been designed (laws of science such as gravity and magnetism, **DNA** being a blueprint for life, etc.).
- If the world has been designed, the world must have a designer.
- The only possible designer of something as wonderful as the universe would be God.
- Therefore the appearance of design in the world proves that God exists.

Catholics believe that the design argument is important because it uses **natural theology** to show that:
- God's existence can be demonstrated by looking at his creation
- God wants humans to use their reason to understand the world as well as the revelation he has given to the Church
- the universe works on fixed, logical principles designed by God which have enabled humans to make scientific discoveries
- God is the creator of the universe and keeps it in existence.

Non-religious people such as Atheists and Humanists reject this argument because:
- the argument ignores the evidence of lack of design in the universe, for example volcanoes, earthquakes, hurricanes, diseases
- all the evidence for design can be explained by science without thinking of God
- the argument does not refer to the existence of such things as dinosaurs which could not have been part of a design plan for the world
- the argument proves only that the universe has a designer, not God. The designer could be many gods, or an evil creator.

The Catholic Church argues that believing the universe came about by chance takes just as much faith as believing it came about through the design of God. It is far more likely that the universe came about through the design of a loving God than through random chance. The Church accepts that there is no absolute proof a creator exists, but argues that there is also no proof that the Creator does not exist. Proof of God's existence is an open question and one which the Church feels comes down in favour of an intelligent designer.

Design When things are connected and seem to have a purpose; for example, the eye is designed for seeing.

DNA A molecule that carries the genetic instructions used in the growth, development, functioning and reproduction of all known living organisms.

Evolution The idea that life forms change over time (humans have developed from amoeba).

Natural theology Knowledge of God based on observation of the universe.

Sources of wisdom and authority

The Catechism says that the existence of God the Creator can be known with certainty through his creation.

St Paul said in Romans chapter 1 that although God's eternal power and divine nature are invisible, they can be understood and seen through the things he has made.

The Letter to the Hebrews chapter 11 says that faith allows us to understand that the world was created by the word of God, so that what is seen was made from things that are not visible.

Now test yourself and Activities answers at **www.hoddereducation.co.uk/myrevisionnotes**

Now test yourself

1 Evolution is:
   (a) The idea that life forms change over time (humans have developed from amoeba)
   (b) When things are connected and seem to have a purpose, for example the eye is designed for seeing
   (c) A molecule that carries the genetic instructions used in the growth, development, functioning and reproduction of all known living organisms
   (d) Knowledge of God based on observation of the universe

2 Natural theology is:
   (a) The idea that life forms change over time (humans have developed from amoeba)
   (b) When things are connected and seem to have a purpose, for example the eye is designed for seeing
   (c) A molecule that carries the genetic instructions used in the growth, development, functioning and reproduction of all known living organisms
   (d) Knowledge of God based on observation of the universe

Activities

Complete the answers to these questions:

1 Outline **three** features of the classic design argument.

One feature is that the universe is a far more complex mechanism than a watch. A second feature is that if a watch needs a designer, the universe must definitely need a designer. A third feature is that _the only being that could design the universe would be God therefore God must exist._

2 Explain **two** reasons why the design argument is important for Catholics. In your answer you must refer to a source of wisdom and authority.

The design argument is important for Catholics because it shows that God's existence can be demonstrated by looking at his creation. As St Paul said in Romans, although God's eternal power and divine nature are invisible, they can be understood and seen through the things he has made.

Another reason is that _God wants is the creator of the universe and keeps it in existence. The catechism says that the existence of God the creator can be known with certainty through his creation_

Exam support

You might be asked to evaluate a statement such as: *'The design argument proves that God exists.'* This table might help answer such a question:

Arguments for	Arguments against
● Anything that has been designed needs a designer.	● The argument ignores the evidence of lack of design in the universe, for example volcanoes, earthquakes, hurricanes, diseases.
● There is plenty of evidence that the world has been designed (laws of science such as gravity and magnetism, DNA being a blueprint for life, etc.).	● All the evidence for design can be explained by science without thinking of God.
● If the world has been designed, the world must have a designer.	● The argument does not refer to the existence of such things as dinosaurs which could not have been part of a design plan for the world.
● The only possible designer of something as wonderful as the universe would be God.	● The argument proves only that the world has a designer, not God. The designer could be many gods, or an evil creator.
● Therefore the appearance of design in the world proves that God exists.	

Topic 3.1.6 The cosmological argument

In *Summa Theologica*, St Thomas Aquinas put forward:

- **The way of motion.** Aquinas argued that things in the universe are in motion but nothing can move unless it is moved by something else, so if things are moving, there must be a first mover, and this everyone understands to be God.
- **The way of causation.** Aquinas next argued that everything seems to have cause and nothing causes itself. An **infinite regression** of causes is impossible, so there must be a first cause to start the process and everyone would call this God.
- **The way of contingency.** All material things are contingent – that is, their existence is not necessary and at one time they did not exist. However, if everything is contingent, then at one time nothing existed, but things do exist, therefore there must be a non-contingent being and everyone would call this God.

Modern form of the argument

- Cause and effect seem to be a basic feature of the world.
- Modern science has developed through looking at causes and effects, and scientific investigations seem to show that any effect has a cause and any cause has an effect.
- This means that the universe, the world and humans must have had a cause.
- God is the only logical cause of the universe.
- Therefore God must exist.

The **cosmological** argument is important for Catholics because it shows that:

- God is the origin of everything: he is the Unmoved Mover, the First Cause, the Non-contingent Being.
- God is not another thing within the universe. God is the source of all being and so has no beginning or end. God is infinite and eternal.
- God is a mystery. Human beings can grasp only so much about God's being and nature.

Non-religious people such as Atheists and Humanists think the argument does not prove that God exists because:

- if everything needs a cause then God must also need a cause
- it is possible that matter itself is eternal and so was never created – that would mean that there would be no need for a first cause because the process of causes could go back for ever
- just because everything in the universe needs an explanation does not mean the universe itself needs an explanation – the universe could just have been there for ever
- even if there was a First Cause, Unmoved Mover or Non-contingent Being it would not have to be the Christian God, it could be the God of any religion.

The Catholic Church responds by arguing that:

- to claim the entire universe 'just happened' is more unbelievable than claiming it was designed and created by God
- the universe is too vast and complex, and works according to too many laws, to have appeared by chance
- our immortal soul is a sign that the universe is more than the material and that it is much deeper than physical laws and can only be explained by God.

Contingency The fact that something does not have to exist; it could either be or not be.

Cosmological Arguing from the nature of the universe to God's existence.

Infinite regression An endless series of causes and effects.

Summa Theologica Thomas Aquinas' major book.

Sources of wisdom and authority

The Catechism says God is infinitely greater than his creation: 'You have set your glory above the heavens.' Indeed, God's greatness is unsearchable.

Now test yourself

1 Infinite regression is:
  (a) Arguing from the nature of the universe to God's existence
  (b) The fact that something does not have to exist, it could either be or not be
  (c) An endless series of causes and effects
  (d) Thomas Aquinas' major book

2 Cosmological is:
  (a) Arguing from the nature of the universe to God's existence
  (b) The fact that something does not have to exist, it could either be or not be
  (c) An endless series of causes and effects
  (d) Thomas Aquinas' major book

3 Contingency is:
  (a) Arguing from the nature of the universe to God's existence
  (b) The fact that something does not have to exist, it could either be or not be
  (c) An endless series of causes and effects
  (d) Thomas Aquinas' major book

4 *Summa Theologica* is:
  (a) Arguing from the nature of the universe to God's existence
  (b) The fact that something does not have to exist, it could either be or not be
  (c) An endless series of causes and effects
  (d) Thomas Aquinas' major book

Activities

Complete the answers to these questions:

1 Outline **three** features of the cosmological argument.

One feature is that because everything is in motion, the universe must have been set off by a Prime Mover – God. A second feature is that everything is contingent which means there must be a non-contingent being (God) otherwise nothing would be here. A third feature is that the universe must have a cause and that could only be God as God is a mystery. Human beings can only grasp so much about God's being and nature.

2 Explain **two** reasons why the cosmological argument is important for Catholics. In your answer you must refer to a source of wisdom and authority.

One reason the cosmological argument is important is because it shows that God is not another thing within the universe. God is the source of all being and so has no beginning or end. God is infinite and eternal. As the Catechism says, God is infinitely greater than his creation: 'You have set your glory above the heavens.'

Another reason is God is the origin of everything - he is the unmoved Mover, the First Cause, the Non-contingent Being

Exam support

You might be asked to evaluate a statement such as: *'The cosmological argument proves that God exists.'*
This table might help answer such a question:

Arguments for	Arguments against
● The argument makes sense of ourselves and the universe because it explains how and why we are here.	● If everything needs a cause then God must need a cause — why should the process stop with God?
● The argument fits in with our common sense. We cannot believe that something can come from nothing and the argument shows that everything came from God.	● It is possible that matter itself is eternal and so was never created. That would mean that the process of causes could go back for ever.
● The argument fits in with science which tells us that every effect has a cause and so the universe (an effect) must have a cause (God).	● Just because everything in the universe needs an explanation does not mean the universe needs an explanation. The universe could just have been there for ever.
● Things must have a beginning or First Cause and the argument explains that God started off the universe.	● Even if there was a First Cause, it would not have to be the God of any particular religion.

Topic 3.1.7 The problem of evil and suffering

Evil and suffering can take two forms:

- **Moral suffering** is caused by humans misusing their free will to do something evil. War is a good example of moral evil: it causes large amounts of suffering and is started by humans who could have chosen differently. Murder and burglary are clear examples of moral suffering. Christians often call actions causing moral suffering sins because they are against what God wants humans to do.
- **Natural suffering** is suffering that has not been caused by humans, such as earthquakes, floods, volcanoes, cancers, etc.

Evil and suffering cause problems for Catholic beliefs about the nature of God because Catholics believe:

- God is **omnipotent** – but if God is all-powerful, he must be able to remove evil and suffering from the world
- God is **omni-benevolent** so God must want to remove evil and suffering from the world because they cause so much unhappiness
- God is **omniscient** and everything that happens is part of his divine plan – which means he must have known all the evil and suffering that would come from creating the universe in the way he did. Therefore he should have created the universe in a different way to avoid evil and suffering.

It follows that if God exists, with the nature Catholics believe he has, there should be no evil or suffering in the world. But as these exist, either God is not omnipotent, or God is not omni-benevolent, or God is not omniscient, or God does not exist.

Why this leads some Christians to examine or reject their belief in God

The existence of evil and suffering challenges Catholic beliefs about God, and as these beliefs come from the Bible and the magisterium it causes Catholics to examine their beliefs, especially when they come into contact with evil or suffering personally. So, if they experience the suffering caused by a natural disaster such as an earthquake, or if their child dies from a disease, they begin to examine their beliefs.

Non-religious people such as Atheists and Humanists cannot believe that a good God would have designed a world with natural evils in it. If they had been God, they would not have created a world with floods, earthquakes, volcanoes, cancers, etc. They find it easier to believe that these features are a result of the Earth evolving by accident from the Big Bang and so they question or reject God's existence.

> **Moral suffering** Suffering caused through actions done by humans.
>
> **Natural suffering** Suffering which is caused by nature and has nothing to do with humans.
>
> **Omni-benevolent** The belief that God is all-good.
>
> **Omnipotent** The belief that God is all-powerful.
>
> **Omniscient** The belief that God knows everything that has happened and everything that is going to happen.

Sources of wisdom and authority

Catechism 221 says 'God's very being is love.'

Catechism 268 teaches that 'God rules everything and can do everything'.

Isaiah chapter 45 says that God is omnipotent, omniscient and omni-benevolent.

Now test yourself

1 Suffering which is caused by nature and has nothing to do with humans is called:
   (a) Natural suffering
   (b) Innocent suffering
   (c) Evil suffering
   (d) Moral suffering
2 The belief that God is all-good says that God is:
   (a) Omni-benevolent
   (b) Omnipotent
   (c) Omniscient
   (d) Omnipresent
3 The belief that God is all-powerful says that God is:
   (a) Omni-benevolent
   (b) Omnipotent
   (c) Omniscient
   (d) Omnipresent
4 The belief that God knows everything that has happened and everything that is going to happen says that God is:
   (a) Omni-benevolent
   (b) Omnipotent
   (c) Omniscient
   (d) Omnipresent

Activities

Complete the answers to these questions:

1 Outline **three** features of the problem of evil and suffering for Catholics.

If God is omnipotent, he must be able to get rid of evil and suffering.

If God is omni-benevolent, he must ....

If God is omniscient, he must ....
....
....

2 Explain **two** reasons why evil and suffering in the world cause problems for Catholic beliefs about the nature of God. In your answer you must refer to a source of wisdom and authority.

Catholics believe that God is omnipotent (all-powerful). Catechism 268 says that God rules everything and can do everything. But if God is all-powerful, he must be able to remove evil and suffering from the world.

Another reason is
....
....
....

Exam support

You might be asked to evaluate a statement such as: *'Evil and suffering are the fault of humans.'* This table might help answer such a question:

Arguments for	Arguments against
● Massive amounts of suffering are caused by wars, which can only be the fault of humans. ● Lots of suffering comes from criminal activity (murder, rape, arson, burglary, etc.), which can only be the fault of humans. ● Suffering comes from diseases which are caused by humans abusing their bodies by smoking, taking drugs and alcohol, over-eating, etc.	● Lots of suffering is caused by earthquakes, which are the result of the tectonic design of the Earth. ● Lots of suffering is caused by hurricanes, which result from the interaction of tropical seas and the Earth's atmosphere. ● Lots of suffering is caused by genetic diseases (cystic fibrosis, Huntington's chorea), childhood cancers, etc., which have nothing to do with humans.

Topic 3.1.8 Solutions to the problem of evil and suffering

REVISED

Christianity responds to the problem of evil and suffering in three main ways.

Biblical responses

- The Book of Job explains how God allowed Satan to punish sinless Job to prove to Satan that Job loved God. Job protested to God, but when he came face to face with God, he realised that God is so great that humans have no right to challenge him. Nevertheless, God has a reason for suffering; it is just too complex for humans to understand.
- The Book of **Psalms** explains that suffering is simply a part of life, but so is joy, and the two go side by side. However, Psalms also claims that suffering can bring believers to a deeper understanding of God.

Theoretical responses

- The **free will** response is the idea that God created humans in his image, so giving humans the freedom to do good or evil, to believe in God or not believe in God. This freedom means that God cannot interfere if humans choose evil, and the suffering which results is the fault of humans, not God.
- The **vale of soul making** response claims that the evil and suffering involved in this life are not a problem because this life is a preparation for paradise. If people are to improve their souls they need to face evil and suffering in order to become good, kind and loving. God cannot remove evil and suffering if he is going to give people the chance to become good. But, in the end, he will show his omni-benevolence and omnipotence by rewarding the good in heaven.
- The good out of evil response claims that suffering may have the purpose of bringing good out of people as they respond to suffering by determining to improve things and ensure that suffering is reduced or even removed.

Practical responses

The main Christian response to evil and suffering is to follow Jesus' example and react in practical ways:

- Christians pray for those who are suffering, asking for God's help through **intercessory prayers**.
- Christians give practical help to those who suffer. Many Christians become doctors, nurses and social workers, for example, so that they can help to reduce the amount of suffering in the world. There are many Christian charities that exist only to help to relieve suffering and remove evil from the world.

> **Free will** The idea that human beings are free to make their own choices.
>
> **Intercessory prayers** Prayers asking God's help for other people.
>
> **Psalms** A book of the Old Testament containing 150 sacred songs.
>
> **Vale of soul making** The idea that God gave people this life to make their souls good enough for heaven.

Sources of wisdom and authority

Psalm 119 says that being afflicted by suffering leads to greater understanding of God.

Job chapter 42 says God is so wonderful that his actions cannot be questioned.

Now test yourself

1 The vale of soul making says:
  (a) Suffering is justified by God giving this life to improve your soul by facing up to real challenges
  (b) Suffering is justified by how God rewards people in this life
  (c) Suffering is justified by God rewarding all who suffer in a future life
2 The book of the Old Testament containing 150 sacred songs is called:
  (a) Song of Songs
  (b) Ecclesiastes
  (c) Lamentations
  (d) Psalms

3 Intercessory prayers are:
  (a) Prayers thanking God for other people
  (b) Prayers blessing the bread and wine in the Eucharist
  (c) Prayers asking for God's help and guidance
  (d) Prayers asking God's help for other people
4 The state of being very moral and spiritual is called:
  (a) Sainthood
  (b) Holiness
  (c) Blessedness
  (d) Martyrdom

Activities

Complete the answers to these questions:

1 Outline **three** different ways in which Christians respond to the problem of evil and suffering.

One way is by using the biblical responses such as those in the books of Job and Psalms. Another way is theoretical, such as the vale of soul making. A third way is practical, such as

....

....

2 Explain **two** biblical responses to the problem of evil and suffering. In your answer you must refer to a source of wisdom and authority.

The Book of Job explains how God allowed Satan to punish sinless Job to prove to Satan that Job loved God. Job protested to God, but when he came face to face with God, he realised that God is so great that humans have no right to challenge him. Nevertheless, God has a reason for suffering, it is just too complex for humans to understand.

The Book of Psalms explains that

....

....

Exam support

You might be asked to evaluate a statement such as: *'Evil and suffering are not a problem for Catholics.'* This table might help answer such a question:

Arguments for	Arguments against
• The Bible shows that God must have a reason for allowing evil and suffering, but humans cannot understand it. • By making humans with free will, God created a world in which evil and suffering will come about through humans misusing their free will. So evil and suffering are problems caused by humans, not God. • The evil and suffering involved in this life are not a problem because this life is a preparation for paradise. • God has a reason for not using his power to remove evil and suffering, but humans cannot understand it.	• If God is omnipotent, he must be able to remove evil and suffering from the world. If God is omnibenevolent, he must want to remove evil and suffering from the world. So if God exists, there should be no evil or suffering in the world. • The world has features that are the fault of God's design — floods, earthquakes, volcanoes, cancers, etc. They cannot be blamed on humans and so cannot be justified. • An all-powerful God could stop evil humans from causing so much suffering, and his not doing so cannot be justified.

3.2 Religious teachings on relationships and families in the twenty-first century

Topic 3.2.1 Marriage

REVISED

The importance of marriage for Catholics

- Catholics believe marriage was created by God as the way of establishing and preserving society.
- Marriage is one of the seven sacraments of the Church.
- Marriage is the only acceptable way for Catholics to have a sexual relationship.
- Marriage is the only acceptable way for Catholics to have children and raise a family.

The purpose of marriage for Catholics is:

- so that a couple can have a **life-long relationship** of love, companionship and **faithfulness**
- so that a couple can have the support and comfort of each other and enjoy sex with each other in the way God wants
- for the procreation of children
- so that children can be brought up in a Christian family and become members of Christ's Church.

The Catholic Church teaches that:

- marriage can only be between one man and one woman (**monogamy**) because this was how marriage was established by God when he created humans
- in the sacrament of marriage God joins the couple in a bond that humans have no right to break, so marriage is for life
- marriage is not for everyone – God calls some people to the celibate life so they can dedicate themselves to serving him as priests, monks, or nuns.

In *Not Just Good But Beautiful*, Pope Francis urged society to return to life–long marriage because:

- the union of a man and woman in marriage is good for both individuals and society
- the family is the pillar which holds society together
- 'children have a right to grow up in a family with a father and a mother'.

Non-religious attitudes to marriage

All Humanists and many atheists believe that it is up to individuals whether they marry or just live together (cohabit), but relationships should be exclusive (only one partner at a time). Many do marry because it gives more stability and legal protection, especially if children are involved.

Most couples now have sex before marriage and cohabit before they marry. Today marriage can be between two people of the same sex.

Catholic responses to non-religious attitudes

The official response of the Catholic Church has been to condemn the non-religious attitude and to insist that Christians should refrain from sex until they have had a Christian marriage. However, a survey by Professor Linda Woodhead into British Catholic attitudes found that 80 per cent of Catholics are in favour of pre-marital sex and 90 per cent are accepting of **cohabitation**.

Celibacy Living without sexual activity.

Cohabitation Living as man and wife without being married.

Faithfulness Staying with your marriage partner and having sex only with him or her.

Life-long relationship The idea that marriage can only be ended by the death of a partner.

Monogamy Marriage to only one person at a time.

Sources of wisdom and authority

In Mark's Gospel, Jesus said that marriage was created by God at the beginning of the world. ✡

In Mark's Gospel, Jesus said that husband and wife are joined by God and 'what God has joined together let not man separate'.

The Catechism teaches that sex must always take place within marriage.

The Catechism teaches that cohabitation is wrong and 'human love does not tolerate trial marriages'.

Now test yourself

1 Christians believe that marriage was:
   (a) Commanded by God in the Torah
   (b) Created by God at the beginning of the world
   (c) Commanded by Jesus in the Gospels
   (d) Commanded by God in the Catechism
2 Living without sexual activity is known as:
   (a) Cohabitation
   (b) Faithfulness
   (c) Celibacy
   (d) Monogamy

3 Living as man and wife without being married is known as:
   (a) Cohabitation
   (b) Faithfulness
   (c) Celibacy
   (d) Monogamy
4 Marriage to only one person at a time is known as:
   (a) Cohabitation
   (b) Faithfulness
   (c) Celibacy
   (d) Monogamy

Activities

Complete the answers to these questions:
1 Outline **three** Christian beliefs about marriage.

Christians believe that marriage was created by God at the beginning of time. Another belief is that marriage is a life-long relationship, so it cannot be ended, for example, by divorce.

A third belief is that marriage
is for the procreation of children.

2 Explain **two** reasons why Catholics get married. In your answer you must refer to a source of wisdom and authority.

Catholics get married because marriage is one of the seven sacraments and as such it is a sign of grace, instituted by Christ himself, and, through the Church, imparting God's grace and strength. Catholics believe they should take part in the sacraments if at all possible and so they feel they should marry.

Another reason Catholics get married is because Jesus said that
in Mark's Gospel, that marriage was created by God at the beginning of the world.

Exam support

You might be asked to evaluate a statement such as: *'Couples don't need to marry to have a happy relationship.'* This table may help you answer such a question:

Arguments for	Arguments against
• Marriage is God's gift (a sacrament for many Christians) as the way humans should have sex and bring up a family. • The Bible teaches that sex should take place only in marriage and that marriage is necessary for the upbringing of a Christian family. • The Church teaches that marriage is the basis of society and that living together without marriage is wrong. • Statistics show that married couples are more likely to stay together than cohabiting couples and that the children of married couples have a more stable and happy life.	• Couples who live together can be just as happy and committed as those who marry. • You can't promise to stay with someone until death if you don't know what it will be like to live with them. • Living together brings all the commitment and joy of marriage without the legal complications. • Weddings are expensive and living together allows a couple to spend that money on the home, children, etc.

The Catholic Church teaches that sex is important because:
- it is a gift from God to be enjoyed by married couples (**unitive sex**)
- sex was given by God so that children could be brought into the world (**procreative sex**).

The Catholic Church teaches that any form of sexual relationship outside marriage is wrong because:
- the Bible says that sex outside marriage is sinful
- the Catechism teaches that **pre-marital sex** is wrong – God intended sex to be restricted to marriage
- adultery breaks the wedding vows to be faithful to one another
- adultery is prohibited in one of the Ten Commandments and is condemned by Jesus in the Gospels.

The Catholic Church teaches that being a **homosexual** is not a sin but that homosexual sexual activity is a sin. Homosexual Christians should live without any sexual activity and the sacraments of the Church will help them do this. The Church does not accept same-sex marriage or civil partnerships because:
- the Bible condemns homosexual sexual activity
- the Church teaches that sexual activity should be procreative as well as unitive – this is not possible for homosexuals
- the Catechism teaches that marriage is for a man and a woman.

However, the Church teaches that it is sinful to harass or attack homosexuals because:
- people cannot help their sexual orientation
- the Bible teaches that everyone should be respected because they are made in the image of God.

Atheist and Humanist attitudes to sexual relationships

Humanists and non-religious people accept sex before marriage and cohabitation because they think that sexual relationships should be up to the people involved. They think that sex should be **consensual**, be between people 'of age' and should not involve cheating on a partner.

Non-religious attitudes to same-sex relationships

Humanists, and the vast majority of atheists, see no problems with same-sex sexual relationships. They regard people's sexuality as their own concern unless it interferes with other people's human rights.

Christian responses to the non-religious attitudes

Some of the Catholic responses were dealt with in the previous topic.

The Catholic Church's official response to non-religious attitudes has been to condemn the non-religious attitude and to insist that Christian homosexuals should refrain from sex and that same-sex marriages should not be legal. This has been confirmed by Pope Francis in his Apostolic Exhortation, 'The Joy of Love', in April 2016.

Most ordinary Catholics no longer follow the official teachings and agree with the non-religious attitudes to homosexuality. Catholic Ireland voted to legalise same-sex marriage in 2015.

Consensual sex When both parties freely agree to sex.

Extra-marital sex Sex outside marriage – usually called adultery.

Homosexuality Sexual attraction to a same-sex partner.

Pre-marital sex Sex before marriage.

Procreative sex Sex which is open to the possibility of new life being formed.

Promiscuity Having sex with a number of partners without commitment.

Unitive sex Sex as a source of joy and pleasure for a married couple.

Sources of wisdom and authority

The Catechism teaches that sex should not be simply biological, the sacrament and commitment of marriage make marital sex 'truly human'.

The Catechism teaches that marital sex should be both unitive and procreative because this is the 'twofold end of marriage'. ✡

Pope Francis said in 'The Joy of Love' that there are no grounds for considering homosexual unions to be in any way similar to God's plan for marriage and family.

Now test yourself

1 Sex before marriage is known as:
(a) Cohabitation
(b) Consensual sex
(c) Pre-marital sex
(d) Extra-marital sex
2 When both parties freely agree to sexual activity it is known as:
(a) Cohabitation
(b) Consensual sex
(c) Pre-marital sex
(d) Extra-marital sex

3 A couple living together in a sexual relationship without being married is known as:
(a) Cohabitation
(b) Consensual sex
(c) Pre-marital sex
(d) Extra-marital sex
4 Sexual relationships between a married person and someone other than his or her marriage partner are known as:
(a) Cohabitation
(b) Consensual sex
(c) Pre-marital sex
(d) Extra-marital sex

Activities

Complete the answers to these questions:

1 Outline **three** Catholic Christian beliefs about sexual relationships.

Catholics believe sex is a gift from God. They also believe that pre-marital sex is wrong. A third Catholic belief is ~~that the adultry breaks that~~ Bible says sex outside marriage is sinful.

2 Explain **two** reasons why many Catholics are against people having sex before they are married. In your answer you must refer to a source of wisdom and authority.

The Catholic Church teaches that any form of sexual relationship outside marriage is wrong because the Bible says that fornication (a word used in religion for both pre-marital sex and promiscuity) is sinful and Catholics should follow the teachings of the Bible.

Another reason is that the catechism teaches that marriage is for a man and a woman + church teaches that sexual activity should be procreative as well as unitive - not possible for homosexuals.

Exam support

You might be asked to evaluate a statement such as: *'Same-sex marriage is wrong.'* This table may help you answer such a question:

Arguments for	Arguments against
● Christianity teaches that God gave marriage for a man and a woman, not two people of the same sex. ● One of the purposes of Christian marriage is for the procreation of children and as homosexuals cannot procreate, they cannot marry. ● Catholics believe homosexuals should not be sexually active and so they cannot accept same-sex marriages because they encourage homosexual sexual activity. ● Pope Francis said in 'The Joy of Love' that there are no grounds for considering homosexual unions to be in any way similar to God's plan for marriage and family.	● A same-sex marriage allows homosexual couples to commit themselves to each other and encourages stable sexual relationships. ● Same-sex marriages are part of giving homosexuals equal rights. ● Same-sex marriages allow homosexual couples to share their belongings, pensions, etc., in just the same way as heterosexual couples. ● Same-sex marriages are a way of encouraging the Christian virtues of love and faithfulness among homosexuals.

Topic 3.2.3 Families

The Church teaches that Catholic parents have a duty to:
- ensure that the **physical needs** and **material needs** of the children are met
- instil **moral values** into their children so that they become good, responsible citizens
- bring up the children in the Catholic faith and do their best to ensure that the children become Catholic Christian adults.

Family life is important for Catholics because:
- one of the main purposes of Catholic Christian marriage is to have children and bring them up in a secure and loving Christian environment
- the Church teaches that the family was created by God as the basic unit of society
- the family is the place where children learn the difference between right and wrong so that without the family there would be much more evil in the world
- the family is the place where children are introduced to the faith and so it is very important if the Church is to continue and grow.

The main family types in the twenty-first century are:
- nuclear families: mother, father and children living together as a unit
- single-parent families: 25 per cent of all families with dependent children in the UK are now single-parent families because of the rise in divorces and family breakdowns
- same-sex parent families: headed by two men or two women
- extended families: three generations (parents, children and grandparents) living in the same house or in close proximity
- blended families: two separate families joined together by a parent from one family marrying a parent from the other family. These families are more common because of the increase in divorce.

Research seems to show the quality of family relationships matters more for children than the type of family.

The Catholic response to different types of family
- The Catholic Church gives its blessing to both nuclear and extended families as both can live within Catholic law.
- Single-parent families need help and are not sinful, so should receive support from the local Church.
- The Church disapproves of same-sex parent families because it teaches that a family should be headed by a married man and woman.
- It disapproves of blended families (unless the parents are a widow and a widower) because the Church does not allow divorce and **remarriage**.
- It disapproves of families headed by cohabiting couples and local Churches should make it easier for cohabiting couples to marry.

Non-religious ideas about the family

Most families in the UK are now non-religious. However, the family is very important to people regardless of religion. Falling in love and having a family is a goal in life for non-religious people who think families should bring up children safely and securely, pass on moral values to the children so that they become good responsible citizens, and provide emotional and financial support throughout life.

Material needs Such things as food, drink and clothing.

Moral values The standards of good and evil, which govern people's behaviour and choices.

Physical needs Such things as housing and shelter from the elements.

Remarriage Marrying again after a divorce.

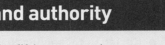

Sources of wisdom and authority

The fifth commandment says that you should honour your father and your mother.

In Ephesians chapter 6, St Paul said that parents should bring up their children in the way of the Lord.

Pope St John Paul II said in *Familiaris Consortio* that Catholics should not live in same-sex parent families, blended families or families headed by cohabiting parents.

Now test yourself

1 Such things as food, drink and clothing are:
   (a) Physical needs
   (b) Essential needs
   (c) Material needs
   (d) Daily needs
2 Such things as housing and shelter from the elements are:
   (a) Physical needs
   (b) Essential needs
   (c) Material needs
   (d) Daily needs

3 The standards of good and evil, which govern people's behaviour and choices, are known as:
   (a) Social values
   (b) Community values
   (c) Moral values
   (d) Religious values
4 Two separate families joined together by a parent from one family marrying a parent from the other family and deciding to marry or cohabit are known as a:
   (a) Nuclear family
   (b) Extended family
   (c) Blended family
   (d) Single-parent family

Activities

Complete the answers to these questions:

1 Outline **three** reasons why family life is important for Catholics.

Family is important for Catholics because one of the main purposes of Christian marriage is to have children and bring them up in a secure and loving Christian environment. Another reason is that the Catechism teaches that the family was created by God as the basic unit of society.

A third reason is

the family is the place where children learn the difference between right and wrong so that without the family there would be much more evil in the world.

2 Explain **two** reasons why the family is important to Catholics. In your answer, you must refer to a source of wisdom and authority.

The family is important to Catholics because one of the main purposes of Christian marriage is to have children and raise a Catholic Christian family. The Catechism teaches that marital sex should be both unitive and procreative because this is the 'twofold end of marriage'.

The family is also important for Catholics because

the family is the place where children are introduced to the faith and so it is very important if the church is to continue and grow.

Exam support

You might be asked to evaluate a statement such as: *'The family is more important for Catholics than for non-religious people.'* This table may help you answer such a question:

Arguments for	Arguments against
• One of the main purposes of Catholic marriage is to have children and bring them up in a secure and loving Catholic Christian environment so that they will come to love God and follow Jesus.	• Many non-religious people see their family as being the most important thing in their lives whereas many religious people see their religion as more important than their family.
• Catholics are taught that the family was created by God as the basic unit of society.	• Most non-religious people have just as good a family life as religious people.
• A Catholic family is the place where children are introduced to the faith and so it is very important for Christianity to continue and grow.	• Non-religious families can respect their children more because they don't have to force them to try to be religious.
• Catholics believe that God will judge them on how well they have brought up their family.	• Religion cannot make a difference to how much parents love their children and children love their parents.

Topic 3.2.4 Support for the family in the local parish

What is the parish?

The Catholic Church is organised in parishes and dioceses. A **diocese** is a collection of parishes under the control of a **bishop**. Each parish is based on a parish church (the church for the local area) and has a **parish priest**.

How the parish tries to help families

- Most parishes have a local church primary and secondary school connected to them providing Christian education and worship in addition to the standard education. This education teaches children about the Christian faith and choosing right from wrong, which helps parents to fulfil their marriage and baptism promises to bring up their children as Christians.
- Many Churches are exploring new ways to be more family friendly, including new forms of family worship which help to unite the family. Often children have their own Liturgy of the Word before the Liturgy of the Eucharist.
- Parishes also help families through **rites of passage**. Priests give advice to the parents before baptism and run classes to prepare children for **First Communion** and later for confirmation, all of which helps parents with the Catholic upbringing of their children.
- Most parish **clergy** spend some time reminding parents of the importance of the family and of keeping their marriage vows, and are available for advice on family or marital problems.
- Parishes provide contact with family help services run by the Church, such as Catholic Marriage Care and the National Catholic Child Welfare Council.
- Family groups are parish friendship groups which bring together people in the local parish with a commitment to know, support and love each other as brothers and sisters in Christ.

Why parishes try to help families

- Parishes try to help families because they have a duty to help children who have been baptised in the Church.
- The Church teaches that one of the main purposes of Christian marriage is to have children and bring them up to love God and follow Jesus, so it is the responsibility of the parish to assist families in that task.
- Catholics believe the family is the most important part of society and that without the family society would collapse, so the parish has a social as well as a sacred duty to help parents with their family life.
- If the parish does not help the family, then Christianity will not grow and the Church will have failed the task God has given it.

Support from the Church is important for Catholic families because:

- raising children as Catholics means taking them to church regularly and that requires the church to be helpful to children
- teaching children about Catholic Christianity requires knowledge and expertise in the faith that parents are not likely to have, so church schools and parish activities are vital
- taking part in the sacraments is essential and that requires the help of the Church
- knowing that the local parish is praying for families brings them God's strength.

Bishop Specially chosen priest who is responsible for all the churches in a diocese.

Catechesis Teaching about the faith.

Clergy Those ordained by the Church.

Diocese A church area under the direction of a bishop.

First Communion The first time a person receives the sacrament of the Eucharist; children receive special lessons before this important occasion.

Parish priest The clergy person responsible for a local church.

Rites of passage Ceremonies marking important stages in life.

Sources of wisdom and authority

The Catechism teaches that education in the faith by the parents should begin in the child's earliest years and the parish is a privileged place for the **catechesis** of children and parents.

In Mark's Gospel, Jesus said, 'Let the children come to me, and do not hinder them, for the kingdom of God belongs to such as these.'

Now test yourself

1 The person who is responsible for all the churches in a diocese is:
   (a) A vicar
   (b) A parish priest
   (c) A bishop
   (d) The Pope
2 What name is given to those who have been ordained by the Church?
   (a) Ministers
   (b) Deacons
   (c) Clergy
   (d) Priests
3 Which of these is not a rite of passage?
   (a) Family worship
   (b) Confirmation
   (c) Baptism
   (d) First Communion
4 Who is responsible for a parish church?
   (a) The bishop
   (b) The parish priest
   (c) The deacon
   (d) The clergy

Activities

Complete the answers to these questions:

1 Outline **three** ways in which local parishes help families.

Most Catholic or Church of England parishes have a local church primary and secondary school connected to them. Also _parishes help families through rites of passage. Priests give advice to the parents before baptism and run classes to prepare children for first Holy communion and confirmation. The parish clergy spend some time reminding parents of the importance of families, marriage vows and parent advice on family problems._

2 Explain **two** reasons why parishes help families. In your answer, you must refer to a source of wisdom and authority.

Parishes try to help families because they have a duty to help children baptised or dedicated in the church and Jesus said _"Let the children come to me, and do not hinder them, for the kingdom of God belongs to such as these!"_

Another reason is _that if the parish does not help the family, then Christianity there will not grow and the church will have failed the task God has given it._

Exam support

You might be asked to evaluate a statement such as: *'Christian parishes help to keep families together.'*
This table may help you answer such a question:

Arguments for	Arguments against
● Many churches support church schools which provide Christian education and worship in addition to the standard education.	● Statistics show that Christian families are just as likely to break up as other families.
● Most parish clergy are available for help with family or marital problems and some dioceses have a special children and family officer.	● Not all Christian churches provide the same level of support; some have few family-centred activities and no youth activities.
● Most church services include prayers for families and for spiritual strength for parents to fulfil their responsibilities.	● Some Christian churches will not provide support for families who have lapsed from the faith or who are having problems over issues such as needing fertility treatments which are banned by the Church.
● Most churches run groups such as toddlers and youth clubs to help parents to bring up their children as good Christians.	

Topic 3.2.5 Contraception

Catholics and family planning

The Church teaches that Catholics should practise responsible parenthood by using natural methods of family planning (**NFP**) and that artificial methods of contraception are against God's intentions because:

- Pope Paul VI's encyclical *Humanae Vitae* declared that the only allowable forms of contraception for Catholics are natural methods
- artificial methods of birth control separate the unitive and procreative aspects of sex, which the Catechism says is not what God intended
- some contraceptives (for example IUD) have **abortifacient** effects (they bring about a very early abortion) and so are against the teaching of the Church
- the Catholic Church regards contraception as a major cause of sexual promiscuity, broken families, the rise in the divorce rate and sexually transmitted diseases.

Natural methods of contraception involve reducing the chance of becoming pregnant by planning sex around the most infertile times during the woman's monthly cycle. This necessitates a couple being in a loving, stable relationship as it requires planning and sufficient love to give up sex at certain times of the month.

Artificial contraception is something that enables a couple to have sex without conception occurring, so allowing the couple to control the number of children they have. It is now estimated that 90 per cent of the sexually active population of childbearing age in the UK use some form of artificial contraception.

Almost all non-Catholic Christians believe that all forms of contraception are permissible because:

sees nothing wrong

- Christianity is about love and justice, and contraception improves women's health and raises the standard of living for children as families are smaller
- God created sex for enjoyment and to cement the bonds of marriage and it is not wrong to separate this from making children
- there is nothing in the Bible that forbids the use of contraception

↳ and church authorities such as leaders of the Baptist have said that contraception is a gift from medical science.

Non-religious attitudes to contraception

Non-religious people such as Humanists and atheists are in favour of all forms of contraception because they assess the rights and wrongs of birth control by looking at its consequences. They use ethical theories such as utilitarianism and Situation Ethics to argue that contraception is a good thing because of its effects which:

- improve women's health and well-being
- raise children's standards of living by preventing unwanted babies
- reduce the need for unsafe abortions
- reduce the number of babies born with HIV
- provide protection against **STDs**, including HIV.

Catholic responses

The Catholic Church has issued statements to Catholic couples that they must use only natural methods of contraception. The Church opposes issuing free **condoms** to prevent the spread of AIDS and sexually transmitted diseases. However, ordinary Catholics seem to have responded by accepting the non-religious attitude.

Abortifacient Bringing about a very early abortion.

Condoms Thin rubber sheath protecting against conception and STDs.

HIV/AIDS HIV stands for human immunodeficiency virus. If left untreated, HIV can lead to the disease AIDS (acquired immunodeficiency syndrome).

IUD Intra-uterine device (the coil).

NFP Natural family planning.

STD Sexually transmitted disease.

Sources of wisdom and authority

Humanae Vitae declared that the only allowable forms of contraception for Catholics are natural methods.

The Catechism says that any methods of contraception which render procreation impossible are intrinsically evil.

The Baptist Church says that contraception is a gift from God via medical science but Christians should avoid contraceptives which take life.

The British Humanist Association says that contraception is a good thing because it makes every child a wanted child.

Now test yourself

1 Which of these are Catholics allowed to use?
   (a) Condoms
   (b) IUD
   (c) NFP
   (d) Contraceptive pills
2 Artificial contraception gives all of these benefits except:
   (a) Improvements to women's health
   (b) Decreases in the number of divorces
   (c) Improvements to children's standard of living
   (d) Decreases in sexually transmitted diseases

3 Non-Catholics allow all forms of contraception because:
   (a) Artificial methods of contraception are banned by the Catholic Church
   (b) Contraception is not mentioned in the Bible
   (c) Contraception puts people off casual sex
   (d) Artificial methods of contraception have always been allowed by the Churches
4 The Catholic Church opposes artificial methods of contraception because:
   (a) They are banned in the Bible
   (b) They prevent the true purpose of sex
   (c) They separate the two purposes of sex
   (d) They are banned in the Creeds

Activities

Complete the answer to this question:

1 Explain **two** different Christian attitudes to contraception. In your answer you must refer to a source of wisdom and authority.

Catholic Christians are against using artificial methods of contraception as they are against God's intentions and separate the procreative from the unitive purposes of sex. Pope Paul VI condemned all forms of artificial methods of contraception in his encyclical *Humanae Vitae*. A different attitude is that of non-Catholic Christians who see nothing wrong in artificial methods of contraception because they are not mentioned in the Bible and Church authorities such as the leaders of the Baptist Church have said that contraception is a gift from God via medical science.

Exam support

You might be asked to evaluate a statement such as: *'The world would be a better place if everyone followed Catholic teachings on contraception.'* This table may help you answer such a question:

Arguments for	Arguments against
Catholic teachings make the world a better place because: • they encourage people to restrict sex to married couples only and cut down on casual sex • restricting sex to married couples would reduce STDs • they are what God wants and doing what God wants makes the world better • Catholic teachings could reduce the number of broken families and the rise in the divorce rate.	Artificial methods make the world a better place because they: • improve women's health and well-being • raise children's standards of living • reduce the need for unsafe abortion • reduce the number of babies born with HIV • provide protection against STDs, including HIV.

Topic 3.2.6 Divorce and remarriage

Catholic teachings on divorce

The Catholic Church does not allow divorce, but it does allow legal separation or **civil divorce** if that ensures the proper care of the children and the safety of the **spouse**. However, the couple are still married in the eyes of God and so cannot remarry. Catholics have this attitude because:

- Jesus taught that divorce is wrong and that marriage is for life
- the couple have made a **covenant** with God in the **sacrament** of marriage which cannot be broken by any earthly power
- the Catechism teaches that a marriage cannot be dissolved and so religious divorce is impossible.

Annulment is a legal declaration that the marriage was never a true marriage and so the partners are free to marry. The Church allows it for such reasons as:

- the marriage was never consummated
- the marriage was not a true Christian marriage because one of the partners was not baptised
- one of the spouses concealed important things, such as they were infertile or had children from a previous relationship. ← *cannot be ended except death of a spouse.*

There can be no remarriage for Catholics who divorce. They are still married and so if they remarry they are in a state of sin (they are committing **adultery**). They may be refused Communion unless they end their new relationship.

Most non-Catholic Churches think that divorce is wrong, but allow it if the marriage has broken down because:

- Jesus allowed divorce in Matthew 19:9 for a partner's adultery
- Christians are allowed forgiveness and a new chance, so a couple should have another chance at marriage
- it is the teaching of these Churches that it is better to divorce than live in hatred and quarrel all the time.

Most of these Churches allow divorced people to remarry, but they usually require them to promise to keep their vows. There is no such thing as annulment in non-Catholic Christian Churches.

Non-religious attitudes

Atheists and **Humanists** believe that all married couples should have the right to divorce if they feel the marriage has failed. Divorce should make sure that the spouses are treated equally and any children are well provided for. They believe divorced people have the right to remarry.

Catholic responses

The Catholic Church rejects non-Catholic criticism and teaches that the non-Catholic attitudes are responsible for the breakdown of family life in modern society. However, Pope Francis has indicated that the Church should adopt a more loving approach to Catholics who have remarried.

Situation Ethics and divorce

Christians, Humanists and atheists often use Situation Ethics to look at issues such as divorce and remarriage. They look at both the advantages and the disadvantages of divorce. Then they look at the people involved and try to work out the best and most loving choice.

Adultery A sexual act between a married person and someone other than his or her marriage partner.

Annulment A declaration by the Church that a marriage was never a true marriage and so the partners are free to marry.

Civil divorce A divorce according to the law of the country but not the Church.

Covenant A binding sacred agreement.

Sacrament An outward ceremony through which God's grace is given.

Spouse Marriage/ cohabitation partner.

Sources of wisdom and authority

Jesus said in Matthew chapter 19 that divorce is wrong unless one of the partners has been unfaithful.

Jesus said in Mark chapter 10 that if someone divorces and then remarries, he or she is committing adultery.

The Catechism says that a marriage concluded and consummated between baptised persons can never be dissolved.

The Catechism says that the remarriage of persons divorced from a living, lawful spouse contravenes the plan and law of God as taught by Christ.

Now test yourself

1 Civil divorce is:
  (a) A divorce agreed to by husband and wife
  (b) A divorce allowed by the Church
  (c) A divorce according to the law of the country
  (d) A divorce that applies in one country only
2 Annulment is:
  (a) A declaration by the Church that a couple are legally divorced
  (b) A declaration by the Church that a couple can remarry
  (c) A declaration by the Church that a marriage was never a true marriage
  (d) A declaration by the Church that a marriage can never end

3 The Catholic Church does not allow divorce because:
  (a) Marriage was ordained by God
  (b) Divorce is condemned in the Bible
  (c) Marriage is a sacrament
  (d) Divorce has never been allowed by the Church
4 Non-Catholic Christians allow divorce because:
  (a) They think it is a good thing
  (b) They think it is often the lesser of two evils
  (c) They think it was commanded by Jesus
  (d) Divorce has always been allowed by the Church

Activities

Complete the answer to this question:

1 Explain **two** reasons why remarriage is a problem for Catholics. In your answer you must refer to a source of wisdom and authority.

Remarriage is a problem because Catholics believe that a Christian marriage cannot be ended except by the death of one of the spouses. The couple have made a covenant with God in the sacrament of marriage which cannot be broken by any earthly power. The Catechism says that a marriage concluded and consummated between baptised persons can never be dissolved.

Another reason is because Catholics believe that Jesus condemned divorce and remarriage when he said in Mark's Gospel *chapter 10* *that if someone divorce and then remarries, he or she is committing adultery.*

Exam support

You might be asked to evaluate a statement such as: *'Christians should never divorce.'* This table may help you answer such a question:

Argument for	Arguments against
• Jesus taught that divorce is wrong and that marriage is for life.	• Jesus allowed divorce in Matthew 19:9 for a partner's adultery.
• The couple have made a covenant with God in the sacrament of marriage which cannot be broken by any earthly power.	• If a marriage has really broken down, the effects of the couple not divorcing would be more evil than divorce itself.
• The Catechism teaches that a marriage cannot be dissolved and so religious divorce is impossible.	• Christians are allowed forgiveness and a new chance, so a couple should have another chance at marriage.
• The Catechism teaches that divorce is immoral because it 'introduces disorder into the family and into society'.	• Many Christians believe that it must be better for families, and especially children, for couples to divorce than live in hatred and quarrel all the time.

Topic 3.2.7 Equality of men and women in the family

but women have a special role as mothers and carers.

REVISED ☐

The Catholic Church teaches that men and women have equal status in the sight of God. However, it also teaches that men and women have different qualities. Since women are the ones with the biological capacity to bring new life into the world, they are also the ones with the caring capacity needed to bring up a Christian family and so they have a crucial role in family life.

Pope Francis has said that women have an irreplaceable role within the family, particularly in handing down to future generations 'solid moral principles' and the Christian faith, but they should also have the right to equal roles with men in the world of work and politics. However, this is not easy for women and the Pope also said, 'The critical question for each woman is to discern the right balance of work, community and family.'

Nevertheless, in most Catholic families, husband and wife have equal roles.

Other Christian attitudes to the equality and roles of men and women in the family

Many Evangelical Protestants teach that it is the role of women to bring up children and run a Christian home. Women should not speak in church and must submit to the authority of their husbands. It is the role of men to provide for the family and to lead the family in religion as only men can be church leaders and teachers. This is based on St Paul's teaching in Timothy that women should not teach or speak in church, the teaching of Genesis 2 about Adam being created first and the disciples of Jesus being men.

completely.

Liberal Protestants believe that men and women are equal and should have equal roles. This is based on the teachings of Genesis 1 that male and female were created at the same time and equally; the teaching of St Paul in Galatians that in Christ there is neither male nor female; and the evidence from the Gospels that Jesus treated women as his equals.

equal status.

Non-religious attitudes to equal roles of men and women in the family

Atheists would tend to have the same attitudes to equal roles as the general non-religious population, which is that men and women are equal and should have equal roles in the family.

Humanists base their beliefs on science and reason, so most Humanists would say they are **equalists** (they believe that men and women are equal and should have equal rights and therefore equal roles in the family). Many of the **suffragettes** and early **feminists** were Humanists.

Equalists Those who believe in, and practise, the complete equality of men and women.

Feminists People who support women's rights because they believe in the equality of the sexes.

Suffragettes Women who campaigned for the right to vote in the early twentieth century.

Sources of wisdom and authority

Genesis 1 says that God created male and female in his own image. ✡

St Paul said in Ephesians chapter 5 that wives should submit to their husbands because the husband is the head of the wife just as Christ is the head of the Church.

St Paul said in Galatians chapter 3 that in Christ there is neither male nor female. ✡

In his 'Letter to the Bishops of the Catholic Church', Pope John Paul II said that equality does not mean sameness – women are the ones with the biological capacity to bring new life into the world and so women have a crucial role in family life.

Now test yourself

1 St Paul says in Galatians 3 that:
   (a) Men and women are equal
   (b) Wives should submit to their husbands
   (c) Men are superior to women
   (d) Woman was created out of man so man is superior

2 St Paul says in Ephesians that:
   (a) Men and women are equal
   (b) Wives should submit to their husbands
   (c) Men are superior to women
   (d) Woman was created out of man so man is superior

3 Those who believe in, and practise, the complete equality of men and women are:
   (a) Humanists
   (a) Evangelical Protestants
   (a) Equalists
   (a) Liberal Protestants

4 Women who campaigned for the right to vote in the early twentieth century were called:
   (a) Emancipists
   (a) Suffragettes
   (a) Equalists
   (a) Humanists

Activities

Complete the answers to these questions:

1 Outline **three** different Christian attitudes to the role and status of women in the family.

The Catholic Church teaches that men and women have equal status but women have a special role as mothers and carers. Liberal Protestants teach that men and women have completely equal status and roles. Evangelical Protestants teach

that it is the role of women to bring up children and run a Christian home, should not speak in church and submit to the authority of their husbands

2 Explain **two** reasons why some Christians believe that men and women should have equal roles in the family. In your answer you must refer to a source of wisdom and authority.

Liberal Protestants believe that men and women are completely equal and should have equal roles in the family. They believe this because Genesis chapter 1 teaches that God created men and women at the same time with equal status.

Another reason is

that Atheists tend to have the attitude, believe that women and men are equal and should have equal roles in the family. Humanists base their beliefs on science, reasoning and also believe in equality of men and women.

Exam support

You might be asked to evaluate a statement such as: 'Men and women are completely equal and should have completely equal roles in Christian families.' This table may help you answer such a question:

Arguments for	Arguments against
• Genesis 1 teaches that male and female were created at the same time and equally. • St Paul says in Galatians that in Christ there is neither male nor female. • There is evidence from the Gospels that Jesus treated women as his equals. • Pope John Paul II and Pope Francis have taught that women should have equal status.	• Pope John Paul II taught that equality does not mean sameness and women's biological function gives them a special role in the family. • Pope Francis has taught that women have equal status, but women have an irreplaceable role within the family. • Many Evangelical Protestants teach that it is the role of women to bring up children and run a Christian home based on Paul's teachings in Ephesians. • Evangelical Protestants believe it is the role of men to lead the family in religion as St Paul said in 1 Timothy that women should not teach or speak in church.

Topic 3.2.8 Gender prejudice and discrimination

The Catholic Church opposes gender prejudice **and** gender discrimination because:

- Genesis 1 teaches that God created both men and women in the image of God
- St Paul taught in Galatians that men and women are equal in Christ
- the Catechism teaches that men and women are equal and should have equal rights in life and society

Vatican II led to pressure from Catholic women for greater equality in the Church, resulting in:

- women being able to study and teach in theological colleges
- women being **extraordinary ministers** of Holy Communion
- women being able to read the Bible readings at Mass (lectors)
- women taking funerals in certain circumstances

Mary Robinson (former president of Ireland) campaigned for an end to discrimination in Ireland. As a result of her work:

- Irish women can serve on juries
- divorce was legalised in Ireland
- contraception was legalised in Ireland
- homosexuality was legalised in Ireland.

Mary Robinson became UN High Commissioner for Human Rights working for equal rights for all.

Other Christians and gender prejudice

Evangelical Protestants teach that men and women have separate and different roles and so cannot have equal rights. They believe that women should not speak in church, should not teach and must submit to their husbands because it is what God **ordained** in the Bible.

Liberal Protestant Churches are opposed to gender prejudice and discrimination and so have women ministers, priests and bishops because St Paul taught that in Christ there is neither male nor female, the Gospels show that Jesus treated women as his equals, and there is some evidence that there were women priests in the early Church.

Non-religious attitudes to gender prejudice and discrimination

Most atheists and all Humanists believe that men and women are equal and should have equal rights. Humanists believe that it is wrong for religion to be able to discriminate against women and that refusing to ordain women or have women leaders should be made illegal.

The Catholic Church has been accused of gender discrimination because it does not allow women to become priests. The Church has responded to this charge by claiming:

- having men-only priests is not discriminatory because the priest stands in the place of Jesus during the Mass and Jesus was a man
- men and women are equal but their sexuality is not interchangeable – people's gender is not an accident
- Jesus chose 12 men and no women to be his apostles.

Extraordinary minister
A non-ordained man or woman who assists the work of priests.

Gender discrimination
Treating people differently because of their sex.

Gender prejudice Believing that one sex is superior to another.

Ordained Set down by God, or made a priest.

Ordination The act of conferring holy orders (making a priest).

Sources of wisdom and authority

Catechism 1938 says that inequalities between men and women are sinful and contradict the Gospel. Christians should strive for social justice, equity and human dignity.

The Catechism says that only men can be priests because Jesus chose only men as his apostles.

St Paul said in 1 Timothy chapter 2 that women should not teach or have authority over men.

Now test yourself

1 Gender prejudice is:
   (a) believing that one sex is superior to another
   (b) believing the sexes are equal
   (c) treating people differently because of their sex
   (d) stereotyping on the basis of gender
2 Gender discrimination is:
   (a) believing that one sex is superior to another
   (b) believing the sexes are equal
   (c) treating people differently because of their sex
   (d) stereotyping on the basis of gender

3 The act of making a priest is called:
   (a) Sanctification
   (b) Sacramentation
   (c) Ordination
   (d) Elevation
4 An extraordinary minister is:
   (a) A priest with special powers
   (b) A woman who is allowed to do some of the tasks of a priest
   (c) A non-ordained person who assists the work of priests
   (d) A non-ordained person who can fulfil the role of a priest

Activities

Complete the answers to these questions:

1 Outline **three** roles of ministry that Catholic women are able to perform.

One role is that Catholic women are allowed to study and teach in theological colleges. Another role is that they can be extraordinary ministers. A third role is

women are able to read the bible readings at Mass (lectors)

2 Explain **two** reasons why Catholics are opposed to gender prejudice and discrimination. In your answer you must refer to a source of wisdom and authority.

Catholics are opposed to gender prejudice and discrimination because Genesis 1 teaches that God created both men and women in the image of God, and also St Paul taught in Galatians that men and women are equal in Christ.

Another reason is because

the catechism teaches that men and women are equal and should have equal rights in life and society.

Exam support

You might be asked to evaluate a statement such as: 'Christians should never treat women differently from men.' This table might help answer such a question:

Arguments for	Arguments against
• Genesis 1 says that God created male and female at the same time and of equal status. • St Paul taught in Galatians that men and women are of equal status. • The Gospels show that Jesus treated women as his equals. • The Catechism says that women should have equal status and dignity.	• Genesis 2–3 says that Adam was created first and it was the woman who led man astray. • St Paul teaches in Timothy 1 that women should not speak in church, and that they should not teach. • St Paul teaches in Ephesians that women must submit to their husbands. • The Catholic Church teaches that women cannot have equal roles because they cannot be priests since Jesus was a man and chose men to be his apostles.